The Zambia Project is a moving and wildly challenging story about what happens when a group of people are willing to be braided together and collectively captured by a daunting and urgent cause. The result for readers is something quite memorable, quite compelling, and even a bit haunting.

Josh James Riebock
Author of Heroes and Monsters *and* My Generation

The burden of the poor and those who are in need, the empowerment of a younger generation to lead, and the beautiful audacity of turning the world upside down for Christ all intersect in the pages of this transformative book. This book provides a simple, yet profound template for activating students to lead with significance in the 21st century. This powerful model is born out of real-life impact, both for the receivers AND the givers of critical resources and hope to the children and communities of Zambia.

Cory Scheer
Assistant Professor of Nonprofit Leadership, William Jewell College (MO)

There's a world changer that lives inside of every person just waiting to be awakened. *The Zambia Project* is an incredible testimony to what happens when we empower young people and connect opportunity with the deeper question of how to truly live out an authentic, real world faith.

Chuck Cichowitz,
President, Noah's Ark Whitewater Rafting & Adventure Company (CO)

This is a must read story. A Kingdom story, about a group of unlikely people and their leader, whose hearts were captured by what is on the heart of God and moved courageously and radically to make God's love tangible for a group of forgotten people. You will be inspired and moved as you read God's story that happened in a small high school in West Chicago, IL. This book is filled with people who have a heart to change the world and the crazy idea that God will come around people who step out in faith to join Him in what He is doing.

Jeff Klein
Teaching Pastor at Jericho Road Church, author of Q: Big Questions *and voice of* Walk the Way

Once, while with a group of veteran Christian school educators, the question came up, "What do you say to students who come back from an experience all charged up wanting to change the world?" Predictably one answer was, "Tell the students their only job right now is to focus on their studies." I wanted to scream "No, No, No!" Our job is to never get in the way of God's leading in anyone's heart at any age. We should pray the dreams of our children and students are outrageously and audaciously large. As you read this incredible story of changed lives, both in Africa and the U.S., don't miss what is often one of the most important ingredients in any Kingdom movement. It was pure joy to watch how God uniquely equipped the mind and shaped the heart of Chip Huber, God's chosen spiritual guide in this amazing journey, to open doors and clear paths for motivated hearts. Read and celebrate this particular story of how God filled the hearts of young people to move now and become his instrument in the lives of others in this moment in history.

Jon Keith
Principal/Chief Operating Officer, Wheaton Academy (IL)

Most of the time, I find myself thinking... there's no way a book can be as good as these endorsements say. But when it comes to this unique partnership between Wheaton Academy in Chicago and Kakolo Village in Zambia, it doesn't take long for one to realize that this is a rare and true story that will be talked about for years to come. I've heard some of the stories, seen some of the photos, and learned about the direct impact this relationship has had on thousands of people. The words on these pages will encourage and inspire you like very few can.

Joe Trost
Chicago Tribune/ESPN.com

Chip Huber writes with insight and passion about a fascinating account of social and spiritual change in the lives of Africans and Chicagoans alike. His story crosses through the barriers of parched classrooms into compassion-filled hearts that only the Holy Spirit can breach, getting at the heart of Biblical justice today and addressing the split between gospel words and humanitarian deeds. More than a definitive story about a relationship with a small community in Zambia, Huber shares a compelling outbreak of the Kingdom of God through a group of high school students that take Him at His word. Read this inspiring story!

Steve Ivester
Director of Student Activities, Wheaton College (IL)

In this book, Chip Huber has crafted a compelling account of what happens when the inherent potential of student leaders is matched with the great needs of our world. After personally observing the Zambia Project unfold throughout the past ten years, it is obvious to me that Chip's vision for student leadership is among the most effective models in existence. Chip's heart beats for God's people in Zambia. In the same way, the heart of this book serves as the drum beat to which leadership development programs in Christian schools and churches should consider marching to if they desire to change this world in the same way that Chip and his students have.

Matt Ridenour
Social Studies Teacher, Minnehaha Academy (MN)

What leaders are saying about

THE ZAMBIA PROJECT

For all of us who tend to stay stuck in our own little corner of the world...this book is a real eye opener. My friend and colleague Chip Huber thought that he was bringing life changing blessings to Zambians only to find that God was using the Zambians to stretch his faith and change his life! This book reminds us in a riveting way of the reasons that God has called us to live beyond the boundaries of ourselves and our familiar surroundings! A must read!

Dr. Joe Stowell
President of Cornerstone University (MI)

A powerful testimony! Chip Huber is willing to allow Jesus to mess up his own life in order to transform the lives of others. The world needs more Chip Hubers.

Rich Stearns
President of World Vision US and author of The Hole in Our Gospel

The students of Wheaton Academy are rock stars to hundreds of kids around the world! Chip Huber's passion for leadership development transformed young leaders in Kakolo, Zambia, West Chicago, Illinois, and wherever their story has been told. He did so by bringing communities together to build relationships and to play soccer. And in the meantime, they raised hundreds of thousands of dollars, built schools, and provided food for the hungry and water to the thirsty. Children all over the globe now say "Just do it"!

Mike Mantel
President & CEO of Living Water International

In a lifetime, few will have a chance to witness a revolution of change. I did not realize that's what I was witnessing when I first spoke to the students at Wheaton Academy in 2003. The power to make a difference lies within us all, and you will find in this book where there was suffering, beauty and true love did prevail. Hope wins. You need to read on.

Princess Kasune Zulu
World renowned HIV and AIDS advocate, author of Warrior Princess, *and Founder of Fountain of Life nonprofit organization*

Chip's book is a kaleidoscope of testimonies and insights into the power of God unleashed through our 21st century young people. This book will be a real encouragement to students and the leaders that work with them.

Dr. Gene Frost
Head of School, Wheaton Academy (IL)

Everywhere I go these days, people are talking about reciprocal, long-term relationships between North American Christians and Christians in the developing world. But Chip Huber has actually done it...and he keeps doing it. This book is the perfect way to chronicle his many years of facilitating true partnership between Midwest students and a Zambian community.

Dr. David Livermore
President of the Cultural Intelligence Center and author of Serving with Eyes Wide Open *and several other books on cultural intelligence and global leadership*

Narratives have within them a powerful ability to stir our thinking, shape our outlook, and awaken our imaginations. *The Zambia Project* is a fantastic example of that reality, with gorgeous implications for youth workers, educators, parents, and development workers. When you read Chip's book, you can't help but think, "Well, clearly, God moved in that situation." But the thing is: God wants to move in and through you also.

Mark Oestreicher
Partner, The Youth Cartel

Chip Huber's Project Lead students came to me in my role as Wheaton Academy Headmaster and told me that they wanted to raise money for a World Vision Project—a schoolhouse. Thinking that their goal was "impossible," I suggested that they should pursue other more common World Vision items—a cow, a goat, or a sheep. The students insisted on a schoolhouse. I told them that I would think and pray about it. God convicted me of my lack of faith and the next day I told the students to "Go for it" . . . and gave them a check for the project. Many observers have watched the Zambia Project become one of the most exciting and well run service initiatives they have ever seen.

Dr. David L. Roth
Chief Education Officer, Christian Heritage Academy (IL)

For the past seventeen years I have watched Chip do transformational work in the lives of students. He has given his life to see students passionately pursue God and lead in His Kingdom. Through *The Zambia Project* you will see how student leaders were able to mobilize a community to reach the least in another continent. Chip knows what students can do, and after reading this book you will too.

Doug Franklin
President of LeaderTreks and author of The Disconnect: Bridging the Youth Pastor and Senior Pastor Gap

Chip is a role model of what it means to lead the next generation to help change the world. And *The Zambia Project* is the manual. Imagine if every high school, college, and church acted this way—the world would look very different.

James Pedrick & Kurt Rahn
World Vision ACT:S

THE ZAMBIA PROJECT

A portion of the proceeds from this book will go to support
Wheaton Academy's Orphan Project in Haiti and
Cornerstone University's Night of Nets Malaria Campaign in Zambia.

THE ZAMBIA PROJECT

CHIP HUBER

FOREWORD BY
STEVE HAAS

THE STORY
OF TWO
WORLDS
FLIPPED
UPSIDE
DOWN

Scripture taken from the Holy Bible, New International Version® (NIV®). Copyright © 1973, 1978, 1984, 2011 by Biblica, Inc. All rights reserved worldwide. Used by permission.

Scripture quotations are taken from the Holy Bible, New Living Translation (NLT®), copyright ©1996, 2004, 2007 by Tyndale House Foundation. Used by permission of Tyndale House Publishers, Inc., Carol Stream, Illinois 60188. All rights reserved.

Scripture quotations are from The Holy Bible, English Standard Version® (ESV®), copyright © 2001 by Crossway, a publishing ministry of Good News Publishers. Used by permission. All rights reserved.

Scripture quotations from THE MESSAGE. Copyright © by Eugene H. Peterson 1993, 1994, 1995, 1996, 2000, 2001, 2002. Used by permission of NavPress Publishing Group.

Religion / Christian Life / Social Issues

ISBN 13: 978-1-4750-0987-3
ISBN 10: 1-4750-0987-9

CONTENTS

:

ACKNOWLEDGMENTS

I have so many people to thank who made this story come alive...

Wheaton Academy students...thanks for falling in love with a community on the other side of the world.

Wheaton Academy parents and families...thanks for loving our family and supporting your kids' dreams.

Wheaton Academy faculty...thanks for your friendship and partnership for so many phenomenal years. So many of you blessed me in ways you can never imagine.

Jon Keith and David Roth...thanks for being open to new ideas and always empowering me as I discovered what God created me to do.

All my former Project Lead students...thanks for acting upon the Spirit's leading in your life and for our friendships that continue today.

Martha...thanks for being a true partner in God's work in the lives of our students and the world in every possible way.

Jeff Brooke...thanks for being the one to carry on and even move to the next level so many things in my worlds of teaching, coaching, leadership, and global engagement.

Doug Franklin and LeaderTreks staff...thanks for embedding in me and hundreds of students a love for serving as a Christlike leader and for a special place to write many of these words.

Bill Shuman...thanks for helping me believe that God had big dreams for my life through your words and taking risks in giving me leadership opportunities before I was qualified to do so.

Cory, Matt, and Chuck...thanks for creating experiences in the Rockies that allowed us to believe we could impact lives below.

Bethel soccer guys...thanks for over twenty years of friendship and community that fuels one another's pursuit of Jesus.

Joe Trost...thanks for helping us use soccer in Chicago to change the lives of soccer players in Africa as you provided a unique platform for our project.

Brandi...thanks for making the West Chicago Starbucks a place where I wanted to write the Zambia story and we could help change the lives of Zambians in a coffee shop thousands of miles away.

First Zambia LEAD team...thanks for chasing a God-sized vision that would change thousands of lives because of your faith and perseverance...and for blazing the trail and the way to Africa.

Stephan and Greg...thanks for the best gift I have ever received in a soccer field in an African village.

Ryan...thanks for thousands of conversations and memories on this surprising journey that messed up both our lives. So, so glad to travel these roads together over the last fifteen years.

Fordson...thanks for dreaming with me about what God might want to do in Zambia as you always took great care of us in our home away from home.

Steve Haas...thanks for being a mentor who always opened rather than closed doors in my life and this story.

Tony Frank...thanks for always going outside the box to help us seek to care for the kids of Zambia and for traveling with me to Africa as a friend and brother so many times.

Unto team and Los Alcarrizos community...thanks for giving me and my Cornerstone University friends the chance to find another place in the world to partner with God in the Dominican Republic.

Cornerstone community and Spiritual Formation staff...thanks for welcoming us and for believing so deeply that college is a time to discover what it means to change the world in Jesus' name.

ACTS Group at Cornerstone University...thanks for giving me a place to talk about and act out my passion for justice every week.

Athletes at Cornerstone University...thanks for being willing to go overseas to use your gifts on behalf of the gospel and for supporting me in getting this book done in a remarkable way.

Soccer Guys at Cornerstone University...thanks for being a community that has truly given me a home in west Michigan as we together pursue God's best on and off the pitch.

Mark Bell...thanks for your friendship and courage and passion for the things I care deeply about. I wouldn't have gotten to the finish line without you.

Zamtan ADP staff...thanks for treating us always like we were fellow Zambians.

Kakolo Village Community...thanks for demonstrating hospitality and gratitude in a biblical way we had never seen before.

Jon McGrath...thanks for bringing words and thoughts alive, and for figuring out how we could make this book move from my computer to its published state in a beautiful way.

Rod Wortley...thanks for helping the right stories and ideas to end up in the book.

Brad Ogilvie...thanks for sharing your life and story with me as you helped me to discover the significance in responding to HIV right around me.

My parents and siblings on both sides of our family...thanks for your enthusiasm and unconditional love that truly is a foundation in my life.

Olivia and Trey...thanks for giving me joy and love every day and for letting Zambia and its children grab hold of your hearts. Can't wait to show you Kakolo Village someday soon.

Ingrid...thanks for being my best friend and for walking this unexpected road by my side, for allowing me to give lots of time and energy to this project without getting bitter about what I was missing, for being willing to live a life of new experiences, for believing this story was worth living and sharing, and for modeling every single day for me what love for those who are hurting and in need looks like as a nurse, mom, wife, and friend.

I WAS WRONG!

by Steve Haas, Vice President and
Chief Catalyst, World Vision USA

It was my first meeting with the summer season's wave of World
Vision interns. Every year our organization gathered an eager collection of college student leaders selected from the finest US and
European universities. Each week, a World Vision leader engaged the
group in an extended time of personal testimony and discussion—a
perk for the eager students as well as invited senior executives. With
little advance notice of the appointment, I had to admit to a level
of disorganization, unusual for me when approaching any group of
more than five or six.

The large audience of young leaders were attentive and confident,
their demeanor enthusiastic, seeking to engage in conversation on
many of the development issues my story touched upon. And then we
broached the subject of AIDS. To be fair, I'm not certain whether the
group surfaced the topic or I did. A fresh face to the global agency's
staff and in my position for only a few months, I was still swimming
in the mind-numbing world of the devastating global statistics that
is the AIDS pandemic. Considering the fact that nearly thirteen million children were orphaned by the virus and the numbers were rising
(with AIDS mortality rates equivalent to fifteen to twenty full 747
jetliners crashing every day for an entire year), was it any wonder I
deemed the virus a hot talk topic?

Encouraged to challenge the group, I asked a male intern sitting placidly a question relating to his generation's engagement in this, the largest of all humanitarian disasters in history. Hearing no answer, I repeated the question seeking to hear his views and the importance of his generation's response. Still the return was an uncomfortable silence, and it was then that I lost it.

Something inside of me broke. What spewed from my lips was nothing less than an in-your-face, intense, take-no-prisoners rant, giving full vent to my personal disappointment that the current "younger" generation was little different than my own in attaching itself to the great causes of our day. I was as surprised with what poured out of my mouth as the students were.

I remember little of what I said except the kicker prior to winding things up and concluding the session, "Tragically, there is only one generation worse than yours in engaging the serious issues of our world with the compassionate care of Christ...that generation is my own and the biggest reason why you have the current AIDS situation as it is."

Student eyes avoided contact, and color drained from more than a few faces. The room went deathly still and the collective silence confirmed what I had privately suspected all along...this generation couldn't be counted on.

I was wrong! *Dead wrong!*

Somehow I had lost contact with God's unique way of exhibiting His greatness. I had forgotten that in Scripture, we discover God's love affair with "smallness," commonplace beginnings, easily overlooked things and people. Benjamin was the most insignificant of the twelve tribes, the runt of Jesse's litter confronted Goliath, Samuel was just a boy when he started interpreting God's messages, the disciples could hardly have been considered anyone's dream team. Even the metaphors for God's present Kingdom—wind, leaven, water, seed, light—seem small in size but overwhelming in their ability to penetrate and transform. In His mastery of all things, God seems to relish the opportunity to profile His glorious strength by using a plethora of the minute and miniscule.

A short time after my inopportune outburst with the interns, I accepted an invitation to speak at a high school showing up repeatedly on the World Vision radar. Second-hand accounts extolled the school's creative AIDS activism and the level of financial resources being raised by teens. The subject of many reports and the pied piper of this particular campus was a successful soccer coach named Chip Huber, who challenged his high school charges to deeper spiritual devotion, in part by forming a connection to Zambian children and their community. Friends who knew of the school spoke of a profound transformation impacting almost every student who walked its halls.

What surprised me in the first of numerous visits to the Wheaton Academy campus was not only the veracity of those initial reports, but that they didn't do justice to a deeper story that was playing out in the lives of these Chicagoland students. These young people were taking on a massive international epidemic by personalizing its objects, while at the same time manifesting a level of leadership moxie completely foreign to me. The ripple effect was impacting siblings, parents, school faculty, and area church leaders. In that initial visit, one hour over a meal with the Wheaton Academy student leaders had me wondering if there wasn't anything they couldn't do.

This isn't to say they haven't had their detractors. When sharing my Wheaton Academy experiences I've been cautioned that Wheaton is one of Chicago's toniest suburbs and that their size of resource procurement for the poor and spiritual devotion are really relative when you consider the opulent bubble in which these students are safely ensconced. Over time I've found perhaps the opposite to be true. Choked by an overabundance of resources, the multiplicity of personal choices, and the need for greater control that "more stuff" brings, maintaining a level of spiritual flexibility is actually more difficult. Jesus was constantly advocating simplicity over complexity when it came to possessions and personal attachments. His challenge to a rich young ruler was a call to loosen his grasp on things, to see more clearly his path in godly obedience.

The students at Wheaton Academy were impressionable, excitable, creative, emotive, and energetic just like any other teens in America. Their lives were a loose string of homework, relationships, athletics, and text messages. They dreamed of an exciting future, satisfying relationships, and expected to be considered adults...but something else was obvious in my observations. They had a deep desire to see the truths that are proclaimed in Scripture frame and assist them in engaging the present they're confronted with.

The students at Wheaton Academy weren't waiting for something to happen. Called by Jesus and Coach Huber to advance boldly as agents of compassion and love, they simply had trusted that God's promises are true, moving joyously forward as though unrestricted by the limiting governor labeled "too young" or "unprepared."

This is God's story. It is a true life account of a group of students faithful enough to trust in the Lord's faithfulness, innocent enough to not register the prohibitions to their vision, and energetic enough to throw themselves at one of the most intractable of human illnesses.

Four years ago, I was invited to speak on global issues pertinent to our organization at a Christian college. Following the chapel presentation, I was feted by several professors and the president of the institution. The conversation was shallow in that socially polite way until we got to some of the finer points of my earlier address where I had challenged campus leaders to make AIDS and other social justice issues more a part of their core curriculum.

Sensing opposition to the unsolicited curriculum challenge, I asked the gathering what the prospective student they desired might be looking for in choosing an institution following high school graduation. Great intercollegiate athletics? Tasty food? Superior course offerings? A plethora of extracurricular activities? Like my initial meeting with World Vision interns, the room went far too silent, and in the quiet, the Lord helped me find my voice, "If you want to serve as a platform for the launch of future leaders, stand apart from other like institutions. You're going to have to allow students to lead *now* on the greatest issues of our day. You're going to have to mobilize personnel and resources to unleash their leadership potential *while* they're in college—if you want world-changing students like Wheaton Academy grads to go here."

A month after my less than glorious meeting with the World Vision interns I was invited to an appointment set by three students who had been in that particular session. The leader of the troika was the same male collegian who had refused to answer my AIDS query which had lit the fuse to my unsettling powder keg. After a round of short introductions, the student laid out his business plan for a new program that would take the AIDS topic to their campus and over time to their peers at other university campuses. That program was called Acting on AIDS (now "act:s," www.worldvisionacts.org) and is on over three hundred US university and college campuses. Coach Huber and many Wheaton Academy graduates are leading some of these chapters across the country.

CHAPTER 1

TWO WORLDS BEGIN TURNING UPSIDE DOWN

As we got out of the van and started to walk across the dusty African landscape, hundreds and hundreds of Zambian adults and children greeted us with chanting, singing, and dancing as a community of passionate and thankful people met our eyes and ears. Our small group of American students immediately became part of the Kakolo community as they hugged and wept with the very people they had only seen in e-mail attachments and PowerPoint slides. The Maposa Basic School in Kakolo Village, the first educational structure ever built by and for these people (with resources provided by students at Wheaton Academy involved in a global fundraising project), helped in a most unusual way to strengthen the faith of a community devastated by the AIDS pandemic in sub-Saharan Africa and a community of suburban Christian high school students struggling to figure out how to live life as Christians in the midst of great blessing from their heavenly Father.

This particular life moment created an indelible memory. It became a turning point, a game changer, a defining experience that flipped upside down the lives of those who never dreamed they would be present for a moment like this one. I specifically remember Laura

Finch, one of our students, telling me that this day was one of those days she would always remember as she looked back at the whole of her life, ranking up there with her high school graduation or wedding day. And it was a day that forever changed and connected the lives of students on both sides of the world.

You couldn't pick two places in the world with less in common to the naked eye than the campus of Wheaton Academy in West Chicago, Illinois and the dirt paths of Kakolo Village, Zambia. One is filled with the finest of luxury vehicles and the other has a handful of bikes parked outside thatch-roof huts. One has immaculately landscaped grounds including a picture-perfect soccer pitch and the other has dirt that blows all over everyone and everything when the wind whips across the dry and barren ground. One is populated by teenagers dressed in the latest fashion wear and the other has children wearing the same outfit every day for a month. One has the latest technology available to almost every person walking the halls and the other does not have a computer or television in sight. Yet both of these places are communities that need something that strangely the other community can provide as God miraculously connects them together.

Over the past ten years of relationship with the needs and the people of Zambia, I've watched God do something remarkably unusual in our midst and in my own heart. Here's a little background to the story of what God has done.

CHIP: I can remember driving through eastern Colorado with a van full of sleeping students on a bright June morning when the thought came again to me: perhaps this next school year will be different than any of the ones I've spent working with and discipling high school students. We were on our way home from a leadership week in the mountains of Colorado and I had an initial sense that God's Spirit wanted to do something outside the norm with his group of gifted and passionate young followers of Jesus. I was well into my second decade of ministry with students and I had thoroughly enjoyed my time and ministry with some of the most amazing teenagers in the world. I had been at a great local church youth ministry before coming to Wheaton Academy as the school's chaplain. To be honest, I'd loved my students and we'd had a lot of great experiences and opportunities in a wide variety of ministry settings. I hadn't had a "perfect" youth ministry experience, but the past decade had been nothing short of enjoyable and fulfilling.

However, there was this sense that in all the missions trips, wilderness adventures, and small group times we were still doing pretty much the expected suburban evangelical youth ministry stuff. I felt like there wasn't much of the supernatural or dynamic activity of God's astounding Holy Spirit I'd read about in the book of Acts. We gravitated toward doing things we could plan and prepare for and do reasonably well. We had spent several evenings in the mountains discussing and praying about many of these kinds of good, but "doable" ideas for the upcoming school year. And despite their validity, our final prayer time was spent daring to ask God for more, for something bigger than we could consider or dream about at this time and place. So we headed back to the urban flatlands without a tangible plan for the next year's ministry calendar, but holding onto a dream that God could change us and perhaps challenge us beyond anything we believed we could do as a team of high school students and their suburban high school teachers. Little did we know that in the year to come God would answer that prayer and do something in our hearts and our community that was way, way beyond what we could dream of under the Rocky Mountain sky. This is the story of how lives were revolutionized and transformed through a Christian high school's involvement with an initiative initially dreamed up by the Christian organizations Youth Specialties and World Vision ironically called One Life Revolution.

LAURA FINCH, 2003 WHEATON ACADEMY GRAD: I wish I could say that the Zambia Project began because we finally came to our senses and realized that millions of people were dying from a preventable epidemic. But really, there is no reason any one of us would have sought out the issue of AIDS to take over our senior year of high school. This was before any of us had heard of the fabulous musical RENT, before (PRODUCT) RED had hit the shelves, before Bono had appeared in the White House garden with an AIDS agenda. Frankly, in 2002 the issue was much too far removed from us to have come up with any such idea on our own. Truly, it started with an afternoon of silence and solitude on a grassy hill overlooking a lake in Colorado.

As Chip has mentioned, we were in Colorado on a five-day hiking and camping trip designed by our friends at Noah's Ark to build team unity in the splendor of the mountains. We were an enthusiastic group, for sure. It was a lot of leaders to have all in one place, and we came from every nook and cranny of the school. The personalities and temperaments in the group were probably as diverse as you could possibly find in one group of people. On the long van drive, there had been plenty of silly moments recorded in a quote book and later, after the trip was over, we strung them all together and printed them onto one of those awful high school T-shirts that nobody wears anymore. But I do remember Chip commenting once that the inside jokes were a sign of a healthy group dynamic.

The agenda for our third day on the trail was to take it easy—hike through the morning, have lunch, and then pick a spot to spend the afternoon for an extended quiet time. It was halfway through the week and having spent the first three years of high school sitting behind a music stand, I was ready for a break. We split up and everyone found a spot to soak in Scripture and pray for a span of four hours. I had never done that, but found it luxurious, and I think the others did too. Afterwards we gathered to make dinner and discuss our solo time. Nobody had anything too specific to say, but the general feeling at the campfire was one of restlessness. "Let's make this year different," someone said, and we all agreed. We headed home with that feeling but no clear answers on what it might ask us to do.

The Project LEAD year was anchored around biweekly, Thursday night book discussions/planning meetings in students' homes. These were held usually in the basement of the home, and were always preceded by some variation on the classic salad/lasagna/brownies dinner. The Zambia Project was "born" at one of these meetings on a chilly evening in November.

CHIP: We were headed to one of the Project LEAD team homes for dinner when I grabbed the latest *YouthWorker Journal* issue in my mailbox at school. I saw an article written by my friend Mark Oestreicher about the AIDS pandemic in Africa, and it proposed a new project where students in youth groups were challenged to raise one million dollars in one year to specifically help respond to the immense needs of children orphaned by the disease in the AIDS-ravaged country of Zambia. I went to the website for some more specifics on the need and project, and I decided I'd bring it up at our upcoming meeting. You see, there were two things that sparked interest in my mind and heart. First, we were still praying and searching for that vision for the school year we had begun asking God for over four months ago. The AIDS crisis seemed to offer a need that was truly enormous in size and scope and significance. Second, one of the girls on our team had spent most of her life living in Zambia and had firsthand knowledge of the people and needs in that particular African nation.

When I passed out information about the project I sat and wondered what their response would be to this new idea. After all, I was quite certain there weren't too many evangelical students or church leaders in their worlds who had talked about or promoted the need for them to engage with or even care about the issue of AIDS and its victims. Little did I know that the church's seeming indifference to the AIDS crisis would be one of the things that made this cause most attractive to this student group. The team immediately voiced that this opportunity was different than the other ones they had looked at and discussed. We sensed that God's Spirit was calling us to be a part of the response. We couldn't resist the leading and the voice of the One who created and longed to save the children of Zambia. As you can imagine, I was thrilled with the heartfelt compassion I saw in the eyes of my students in that basement. I silently thanked God for the joy and privilege of working with and walking alongside this amazing group of friends.

LAURA: We had our usual discussion on a chapter by Henri Nouwen or Andy Stanley or another Christian leadership guru, and then Chip pulled out a stack of these World Vision catalogs. You know, the kind that come out right before the holidays and feature gifts to send overseas where they are really needed, as an alternative to buying more items to clutter the lives of your loved ones. This particular catalog was focused on items needed by communities suffering in the grip of the global AIDS pandemic. He suggested that we take a look and consider picking one or two items to hold a fundraiser for as a school initiative. It was a fresh and appealing idea that we couldn't remember trying before at Wheaton Academy, and we eagerly flipped through the colorful, glossy pages, pointing out the unique gifts that were available—a pair of chickens or goats, a set of warm blankets, a year of school supplies for a child. Someone pointed out that the cost of a brand-new house was only $3,000. Someone else pointed out an item with a price tag of $10,000. The dreaming muscle started to twitch. Surely that could be done with a few fundraisers, right? It was little more than the cost of a typical missions trip many of us had been on. That would be a good project. It would definitely keep us busy for the year.

Looking back, this was probably one of the pivotal moments of the project, although it certainly didn't feel that way. We were already sold on the fundraiser idea. We had already set a challenging, but realistic goal. It would have been so easy to close the catalog, eat another brownie, take prayer requests, and go home. But somebody just had to flip to the back page just to see the most expensive thing available.

There it was. A three-room schoolhouse with a price tag of $53,000. The next most expensive item was tens of thousands of dollars less. The World Vision people told us later that's exactly why it had been put in the catalog—it was the out-there, far-and-away item that they didn't expect anyone to buy, but that had to go in because our God is just that big, after all. Sitting there in the basement on that night in November, we had no idea that there was a little village called Kakolo on the other side of the globe which had been praying for a new school for two years. We didn't know that the Zambians being served by World Vision in the Zamtan Area Development Project had been hoping and praying for a new school so that their children would no longer have to walk over six kilometers each way and cross a busy highway on foot just to get an education.

In fact, there was relatively little discussion after it was first noticed. It was just settled. We were a school, and they needed a school. We wanted to initiate something different that year, and here was a ready-made project, picked from a buffet of items from a reputable nonprofit that was obviously a good and worthy goal. The dollar amount probably should have seemed more outrageous to us. The September 11 attack had just begun to take a toll on the economy, and our own school was in the middle of a multimillion dollar fundraising campaign of its own. We knew next to nothing about the AIDS pandemic, and we had no idea that our lives were about to change. But we knew we were supposed to do something more, and there on the catalog page was the opportunity. It just made sense.

CHIP: How does a vision become a reality? That was the rather large and overarching question now facing us as we began to brainstorm ideas for how one goes about raising $53,000 as a group of teenagers. The first step was to tell the rest of the student body about it through conversations with individual friends and then small groups of people like class officers, faculty members, and even the school board. We also prepared a couple of special all-school chapel presentations where we highlighted the incredible reality of the devastation AIDS has brought to the children of Africa and specifically the group of over one million orphans living in Zambia. We used videos highlighting specific families who were victims of the disease, and even used interviews and quotes from the pop music icon Bono who was in Wheaton himself championing the needs of the African continent to Midwest Americans. The students did a very thorough and attractive presentation of the need and opportunity for response, but the initial feedback of their peers and the larger community wasn't quite what they expected or hoped it would be. I would describe the initial reaction to the vision presented as uncertain and rather skeptical in nature. The numbers seemed too sterile, the videos and pictures too guilt-driven, and the AIDS cause in general remained one that American evangelicals still regarded as not worthy of their attention and resources. We had read that people like those involved with Wheaton Academy were among the most unlikely in the world to give money to people infected with HIV/AIDS virus, and we saw those statistics play themselves out in some of the early reactions to the One Life Revolution initiative. It was risky to take public such a grand vision for a somewhat "controversial" cause, but now we had put it out there and had no opportunity to take it back.

Well, as you fast forward, God did show up in our lives and in our school that year. On the morning of May 20, the last day of school for this group of senior leaders, we had a chance to celebrate in an all-school chapel all that God had done, a work that was exactly what He had promised in Ephesians 3:20, something "immeasurably more than all we ask or imagine"[1] as His power and love were at work within us in new and fresh ways. One of the senior girls had made an oversized check to World Vision and filled in the $72,000 amount that was the representation of the very heart and character of God. We presented the check to some of our friends from the World Vision office in Chicago, and I fought back tears as I tried to sum up the past seven months and give thanks and praise to our God and those who had responded to His call. It was one of those moments as a follower of Jesus where you know that it is real, that God is alive and active. You know you have a calling and meaning and purpose in life that is undeniably profound, valuable, and consuming, and that choosing to live life investing what you have been given for the sake of others and not just yourself is indeed the best way to spend your days on this earth.

We ended chapel as a community of worshippers singing about the God who is Lord of all the nations, and I couldn't help but dream of that day yet to come when we would be together to worship with our brothers and sisters from Zambia who will no longer be threatened by AIDS and poverty, but instead will revel in the riches and glory of God for all eternity. In many ways that chapel service could have been the final chapter of our Zambia story. But in reality, our journey was about far, far more than building a school; it was really about responding to the call of God by choosing to live our lives with eyes that see others rather than focusing on our own wants and wishes.

One day in June, I walked into my office and found a couple hundred dollars on my desk that came from a senior student's graduation party. The project was "finished," but the needs of the people of Zambia continued. A year-long project became a lifetime passion and pursuit for many, and we saw up close how spiritual transformation can occur when we enter into relationship with the poor in our world. And over the next several years Wheaton Academy students raised almost three-quarters of a million dollars to help in the physical restoration and spiritual renewal of a generation of African kids.

The evangelical church has struggled deeply in responding to the AIDS crisis and the needs of the poor. In my own lifetime of following Jesus, the message of Matthew 25 where our Savior calls us to personally care for "the least of these" was seldom preached. And, in my over forty years of being immersed in Christian culture and ministry I have rarely been challenged to use my resources and influence to advocate and heal the needs of those afflicted with poverty and hunger and disease around the world. Yet now I am confident that a rather large handful of future church leaders coming out of the suburbs of Chicago will lead God's people in a new direction, one where they will share the love and hope of Jesus to people who are at the greatest risk physically and spiritually on our planet. The Holy Spirit, for some reason only God knows, chose to descend upon this group of teenagers and anointed them to bring a new vision of gospel mission and ministry to this generation and those to come.

So that's what this book is really all about—the stories and words of a group of students and their teachers who fell in love with the people and culture and faith of a community on the other side of the world. As you keep reading, you'll hear more about their journey and the incredible opportunities they have had to travel to Zambia and truly build friendships with those whom God connected them to through simple prayers several years ago. You'll also hear from the Zambian community how they got to know and came to love some rich American kids whose lives looked nothing like theirs in any way. My prayer is that after reading it you'll believe in the anointing of this generation of students to be restorers of God's Kingdom and that you yourself will consider joining God in pursuing the dreams He has for you to be deeply engaged in His work around the world. Enjoy the story. May it reflect God's passion for His people, both in wealthy enclaves like Wheaton, Illinois and poor African villages like Kakolo, Zambia. To Him be the glory and the blessing for bringing these two places together under the umbrella of His great love as He keeps turning lives upside down in the process.

HOW ZAMBIA SAVED MY FAITH

Kyle Pilcher

In a way, I think my trip to Zambia saved my faith. I was so sick and tired of the fake, two-faced Christians in my community, myself not excluded. So many of us take so much for granted when, considering all we have, we should have a spirit of nonstop praise and thanksgiving to our God.

We complain about gas prices when instead we should be thankful we have a car. I can't imagine walking the eight miles I travel to school every morning if I didn't have a car. We complain when we are hungry between meals, when we really should be thankful that we eat multiple meals a day. We complain when places feel overcrowded, when we should be thankful that we don't go to school with six hundred other kids in a space smaller than my garage.

I also wonder why we are sometimes (or all the time) ashamed to be confessing believers in Jesus. The people of Zambia say "God bless you" to total strangers, wholeheartedly meaning it. I have a hard time talking about my relationship with God to even my family and friends. People in Zambia pray over loud speakers in front of strangers, and I won't even pray out loud with a friend at a restaurant just because of the way it looks to others sitting around us. If Wheaton truly was a "church community" then I should be able to walk around talking about Jesus without worrying I'll be mocked or ridiculed.

I guess what I am trying to say is that in some way my faith was faltering because of my disgust with the "Christian community" surrounding me. I became susceptible to all of the things mentioned above, and I steadily grew further from Christ because I forgot His power and the joy I should have in just knowing Him. Seeing the Zambian people have joy in every situation was an incredible experience for me. Every meal is a blessing, every pen, pencil, and notebook is a gift straight from God, every raindrop is sent from heaven, and every plastic bag they find flying around the dirt paths to make a soccer ball is a miracle. Every one of them is so genuine and there is no façade being put up to impress us. They are the most humble people in the world. Their example to me, without them even trying, has left a deep imprint, a real scar on my life. My jealousy of their faith cannot be put into words. I will forever be in debt to them because they showed me the way a true follower of Jesus should act and think, no matter where one lives. My faith is alive again because I met Jesus in Zambia this past summer.

Kyle is a junior finance major at Belmont University in Nashville, Tennessee. He has been involved with United for Change's Blood:Water Mission at Belmont for the last three years.

CHAPTER 2

LIFE AS A SUPER-DUPER EVANGELICAL

On the last school day before I went off on a writing leave to begin this book, I spoke in our Friday chapel service. I was letting the student body know that I wouldn't be around for the next couple of months on campus, and I decided to try to explain to them why I was going to write out the story of what God had done in and through Wheaton Academy students' lives over the last six years. And to try to do that, I chose to tell my story, the very personal, very unlikely story that I never thought I would be typing out on my computer today. I am without a doubt a most unlikely candidate to be at the helm of a long-term initiative focused on responding to the massive global issues of poverty and AIDS. Here's the description I settled on as a summary of the last several years of my life:

> *How a preppy suburban evangelical guy sees God transform him into a broken, social justice-minded AIDS activist who falls in love with a continent on the other side of the world and calls people in a hidden and poverty-stricken community in Zambia some of his best friends—aka being wrecked for the ordinary and the good.*

In fact, the first slide I put up as a title for people to see as they walked in was a somewhat overused but, in my case, very accurate and descriptive phrase "How Jesus Messed Up My Life." You see, to be honest, my life looks nothing like it did in previous decades. When Paul describes himself in the New Testament as a Hebrew of Hebrews (Philippians 3:5) and a card-carrying member of the Pharisee club by birth and in every other way (Acts 23:6), I can relate. I am an evangelical of evangelicals, a participant in and product of almost every evangelical type of program and community that has existed in the last thirty years. My story is enmeshed with the typical stereotypes associated with the modern evangelical movement that has indeed shaped me and given me much of my identity. I have attended and volunteered and worked at not just one, but *seven* different megachurches throughout the Midwest. I was a kid who was present at every retreat, summer camp, mission trip, and Sunday and Wednesday night activity placed in front of me. I was a student small group leader and spent my college summers working as a youth ministry intern and a counselor at a Bible camp in the north woods of Minnesota. And then I achieved the ultimate level of spiritual engagement for a suburban evangelical kid in that I actually served on staff as a high school pastor for almost four years. For me, the local church and its myriad of programs and projects were my social schedule, my network of friends, and the place I called my second home.

But even more than that, I was and still am deeply entrenched in the world of Christian education. I spent much of my free time growing up in the local church context, but also walked the hallways with other evangelical students from eight to three every day. I was the student chaplain at my Christian high school and sat in Bible classes every semester. After high school I headed to the Christian college world where once again I became fully entrenched in just about every type of Christian growth and leadership experience Bethel College (MN) had to offer. I attended a famous Christian author's church in downtown Minneapolis every Sunday and heard hundreds of speakers in chapel over four years. To be honest, I can't imagine that there were many of my contemporaries who were more involved in evangelical stuff than I was during my high school and college years.

After working for a few years in local church ministry, I moved on to become the Spiritual Life Coordinator at Wheaton Academy in the western suburbs of Chicago. As you might judge from my new job title that produced many mocking messages from my youth ministry friends, I was now so indoctrinated in the evangelical message and mind-set that I was now deemed capable of doing the coordinating necessary to help my students to become card-carrying evangelicals who looked just like me. I had settled in the evangelical mecca of Wheaton, Illinois and found myself working at a school that was the precursor to Wheaton College in the historical center of the American Christian universe.

Now I am obviously being a tad overdramatic here, but the reality is that for over thirty years of my life, I was a prime example of a subculture that has dominated the American church in many ways during my lifetime. I ate the evangelical cookies and drank the evangelical Kool-Aid just about every single day. I am deeply thankful for the unique experience of my life in so, so many ways. I grew up with a clear sense of the love of God as the foundation for my life. I met and built friendships with other Christ followers, including my amazing wife, and they have shaped the essence of my character and helped me to steer away from making some painful and potentially harmful life decisions. I was allowed to test and discover and then use my gifts in ways where I was often affirmed and allowed to fail in rather safe environments. And I both heard God's Word and saw it being lived out in ways that caused me to decide that following and serving Christ was indeed the best option for my life. I look back on those days as being ones filled with great memories, significant and meaningful decisions, amazing friends, joy found in ministry, and a life experience that brought me great satisfaction and very little true difficulty or need. It was a *wonderful evangelical life....*

But in 2002, God began to mix things up a bit and those things that so deeply defined me began to be questioned, even in the midst of living in the heart of evangelicalism every day. And when God started to play with the recipe of what being a Christian should look like for me, His movement in my life smacked into years and years of ideas and experiences that had laid a deep and firm foundation of how I viewed my own faith and ministry as a result of my cultural surroundings and norms. Here's a small list of what I would tell you I heard and then took on as fact in those formative years:

Growing in my faith happened mostly through personal growth activities, including a daily quiet time, praying for the needs of others, and listening to sermons and messages given by pastors.

Being a Christian meant that I voted Republican and that I was politically conservative on the issues that really mattered.

There was a rational basis and defense for why I could and should believe in creation, the authority and inerrancy of the Bible, and the resurrection of Jesus. One of the key tasks as a thinking Christian was to know all the proofs for these realities and then be able to defend them intelligently when questioned or given an opportunity to explain to an unbeliever why they should strongly consider becoming a Christian.

Being a globally-minded Christian meant that I would pray for missionaries, support financially those Americans on the field doing God's best work, and travel to tell people outside of America about Jesus.

The ultimate and singular task of ministry was to see other people decide to follow Jesus and pray a prayer of salvation inviting Christ into their lives after hearing the gospel presentation from a Christian explaining it in clear and precise terms with a specific order, consistent format, and standard response.

I then passed on all these things to the students under my leadership as a teacher and pastor. We checked on each other's daily devotional time in discipleship groups and provided handouts for students to fill in the blanks with words for our Sunday morning and Wednesday evening talks. I passed out materials like voting guides from Family Research Council. I taught a breakout session on apologetics at a student evangelism conference called SEMP in downtown Chicago. Our mission trips included the verbal proclamation of the gospel through doing surveys and using tracts in tourist spots in Chicago and New York City, and we hosted vacation Bible schools and sports outreach events in poor communities in Mexico. We spent thousands of dollars running big outreach events where we tried to get non-Christian kids on our church campus so we could play games or do something else fun or crazy before closing the night with an invitation for them to become Christians and become part of our youth ministry.

The fascinating part of my story is not that there wasn't anything at all wrong or unbiblical about what we were trying to do; I just didn't have any idea that there was more to encounter and experience in the Scriptures and life as a follower of Jesus. Perhaps the most unusual thing I have noticed in looking back is that I didn't know anyone else in my evangelical world that was really doing anything different. There was a system that was taught and then replicated across the country with almost universal machine-like precision. I really didn't know or even stop to consider that there might be different priorities or a different methodology that might be acceptable for followers of Jesus to embrace. I found myself moving into a place in life where not only was I continuing to learn and grow in my belief and understanding of what it meant to be an evangelical, but I was now teaching the same values and ideas and strategies to others as I worked with student leaders and youth workers.

I loved what my life and my ministry looked like as a husband, a ministry leader, and a disciple of Jesus. I had found a model that I liked, and my niche in the Christian community felt comfortable, safe, and was being affirmed by those around me. My first thirty-plus years are something that I look back at and treasure deeply.

However, somewhere along the classical evangelical journey that I was blissfully enjoying, God was lurking and moving in the shadows just off that very well worn path. In some moments He was speaking a different language and offering different ideas, sometimes allowing me to see things I wasn't used to seeing in my suburban world framework. Eventually He used other Christ followers to cause me to look at the road map I was using in my life and begin to wonder if there might indeed be another path that I should explore in my desire to walk the road that Jesus walked. As I began to listen to the voice of the Holy Spirit nudging me and as questions began to grow louder and more specific in my mind and heart, slowly but surely, things started changing for this guy who seemingly had it all figured out.

When I was a high school pastor at a large evangelical church in a suburb of the Twin Cities called Edina, I had the first of many moments inviting me to consider this notion that there was a hole in my theology, my ministry focus, and even my heart. This particular youth ministry had a rich tradition and I was following as an insecure and inexperienced twenty-three-year-old in the footsteps of experienced and nationally known youth communicators. I poured myself and just about all of my waking moments into being with and teaching and creating opportunities for growth in my students. Most of my students attended Edina High School and people who went to other high schools believed that the school name stood for "Every Day I Need Attention." Many of my students were wealthy, successful, and privileged.

God had clearly called me at this time in my life to minister to some of the most financially blessed folks in His whole global church body. As a church, we invested deeply in our missions program and our youth ministry had a three or four track system of mission trips we had developed for students. One interesting thing I discovered in the planning process for our specific trips was that you actually got funds and approval from the church missions department if your trip was geared to do certain things. Consequently, all of the high school trips I designed and led were focused exclusively on telling others about the Good News we had found in Jesus Christ rather than any type of work or service project in a community.

Our most popular trip went to Tijuana, Mexico to run a vacation Bible school for children and a sports ministry for kids and men in the surrounding community. After games and crafts and a Bible story in the church where we recruited the neighborhood children to come, we invited them to raise their hands if they wanted to pray a prayer through one of our student translators to become a Christian. All week we played soccer and basketball games against different teams of Mexicans. We had one of our student players share his or her testimony through the help of a local pastor after the game. The team and fans were told to gather and we invited them to join us in giving their lives over to Christ. My students and I really did love being part of this community and we went back to the same place for three years, building relationships with the pastor and a few other adults and teenagers. And when we went back home we reported each time in the Sunday night service how many people had made decisions to follow Christ as a result of our ministry visits.

We actually developed a sort of pride in the fact that we lived in tents on a dirt hillside and ate pretty questionable food cooked by mission agency ladies over the course of our week in Tijuana. Shower opportunities consisted of a garden hose strung over a cement wall and there was a nightly collection of tarantulas to entertain our team after returning from our ministry site. We didn't even visit the tourist spots near the border because we wanted to keep Mexico about ministry rather than our own pleasures. (Although, on the way home we did stay in hotels in swanky Orange County so we could take a swim in the ocean and eat at the local restaurant buffet.)

The ministry organization from the US that ran this site and helped connect us to local churches repeatedly told us not to get involved with meeting the physical needs of the people and communities we went to because we were there to focus on spiritual needs and we didn't want to create a notion that the Americans were here to just bring money and not the gospel. This policy was in alignment with our church mission department's wishes so we didn't really do anything to help meet the needs of a clearly impoverished community. Our church host in Mexico was meeting in a small cement block building attached to the side of the pastor's house. Looking back on it now, their need was truly quite startling and even expressed in multiple ways by Pastor Manuel whom we all considered a good friend and appreciative host.

I guess that seeing the need finally was too much for a couple of my older male students. In what turned out to be our last time visiting this community, they decided to stay back from the sports complex one morning. They secretly took Pastor Manuel out to a local lumberyard and personally bought for him some building supplies to fix the gaping hole in his roof evident every time we entered the church building. This spot, with the hole above, turned out to be the room where his two children were sleeping, and it had been exposed for several months as a result of his small church congregation's meager offerings. No one else on our team, including me, knew that they had paid for the supplies that somehow showed up. I guess the guilt must have finally gotten to them by the end of the week as they came to me late one night and "confessed" to me how they had broken the "rules" by helping him to keep the rain and cold out of his kids' bedroom. I think they said something about the fact that they just couldn't leave this time without doing something because they knew they would most likely never come back to this community, and they had no idea how else it would get fixed.

As I lay down in the backseat of our rental van that night where I was sleeping for the week, I was awake long after our conversation concluded. I remember thinking, "What kind of a youth ministry am I leading when my closest students have to be ashamed to tell me that they provided a roof for an incredible servant of God who just needed a little help to care for his family?" I thought of all the times my heart had been touched seeing the needs of families and people in Tijuana over the course of three different summers. I wondered why I had never bought any building supplies or food or medicines or school supplies with the "emergency cash" the church had given me before I left on the trip. So when I got home I did something no one ever has known about until now. I took out Pastor Manuel's address and I put that extra couple of hundred dollars in cash from our trip into an envelope and sent it off to Tijuana, not knowing if it would ever get to him, but desperately praying that God would use it to help them and their church as I followed the example of my compassionate and courageous students. (I am fully aware now that I violated just about every principle guiding development work in doing this!)

I ended up about six weeks after that final trip to Mexico moving from Edina to the western suburbs of Chicago to take a job at a Christian high school called Wheaton Academy. This high school was positioned for growth and they offered me the job of leading the spiritual life arena at the campus, including teaching Bible classes, running a chapel program, creating service opportunities for students, helping both students and faculty members to grow spiritually, and being a coach in the boys soccer program.

I jumped in with both feet and immediately fell in love with my job and the students at the school. The environment was decidedly evangelical and most of the students were excited about learning more about what it meant to be a committed Christian. It fit my background and skills and interests almost perfectly, and I began a long-term ministry position in the world of Christian education where I had grown up.

We were totally immersed in the Wheaton Academy world, had our friends through relationships with the school staff and families, and even lived on the campus as a family with young children. My job evolved into even more responsibilities and I began to have opportunity with others to create a unique and seemingly compelling Christian school culture. We had discovered a philosophy and methodology that evangelical parents and students responded positively to, and my ministry and life felt settled and productive as we moved into the twenty-first century.

Our school was both very much evangelical and very much suburban. We charged a rather steep tuition to attend and most of our families came from places where nice homes, new cars, and lots of toys were the norm. To be honest, I think we were viewed in the larger community as a religious prep school for rich kids that provided a good education, had a good sports program, and talked a lot about Jesus. In some ways, that perception was reality and that reality seemed to be very attractive as we doubled in size over a ten-year period.

As I continually looked at our student culture and their spiritual condition, a couple of things bothered me in the midst of a lot of affirmation and growth. I struggled with the notion that we were taking wealthy students and turning out future wealthy adults who would follow their suburban blueprint in financial and lifestyle decisions. I was also quite concerned that my student graduates were educated far beyond their obedience. They were being literally jammed full of ideas and Scriptures and facts and truths in classes, chapels, and a host of other cocurricular areas of involvement. It was all good stuff, and education is definitely designed to stretch student minds and give them information that will help challenge and change their thinking patterns and worldviews. But as I entered into my seventh year at Wheaton Academy, I found myself restless, restless enough to look at other jobs, and disturbed enough to begin to pray and ask questions about what I was doing as a Christian educator to truly make a mark on student lives, on our school community, and on the world we were supposedly preparing students to engage and change in their future lives.

Where were the real-life examples of how our graduates and even current students were positively changing the world after receiving one of the best Christian educations money could buy? Where was the tangible proof that Wheaton Academy was clearly demonstrating the love and message of Jesus to those in the world who had the greatest needs? I had now spent over a decade of my life trying to disciple and bring to Jesus a generation of suburban American teenagers who were more than willing to talk about Jesus and who were more deeply committed to chasing the American dream and lifestyle than the generations before them. And if I dared to ask the final exam level question, "Were we changing and transforming lives at a level where they were moved to acts of great faith and impact in the world?" the answer was probably not as positive as I wanted it to be. I truly think God heard me ask these questions, and His responses did indeed mess up, and maybe in some ways wreck my life and hundreds of students' lives forever.

REFLECTION

LEARNING TO SHARE

Martha VanZee

Sharing doesn't come naturally or without resistance for a toddler, even though teaching one to do so is commonly seen as an act of parenting. It is a basic instinct that we as humans have, to protect and nurture our own needs and desires first. Sharing doesn't fit into that mind-set. Ten years ago, my own adult understanding of putting others' needs ahead of my wants and desires was put to the test. I distinctly remember sitting in the basement of a student leader's home where we all decided that we wanted to make sacrifices to raise money to build a schoolhouse in a small village in Zambia. It was clearly the Spirit of God moving among us who gave us the desire to share the financial resources He had given to us, to work for a people group we knew nothing about, except for their desire to have a proper place to be educated.

> "I know that the LORD secures justice for the poor and upholds the cause of the needy" (Psalm 140:12).[2]

I had no idea how that decision to follow God's leading would impact my life. First of all, I learned that God's resources are unlimited. It isn't about me giving up all that I have for another, but rather being a physical representation of God's love to another human being. I have found the more I give to others, the more God has blessed my family and me.

> "Whoever gives to the poor will lack nothing, but those who close their eyes to poverty will be cursed" (Proverbs 28:27).[3]

I also experienced the truth that God's example of sacrificial love propels me to be like Him. As orphans, He adopted us. Not only did He share in our suffering by becoming a man on this earth and dying in our place for our sins, but His blood redeemed us so that we now belong in His family as His very own sons and daughters, that we might be called co-heirs with Christ. My understanding of this truth led me, and my husband, to adopt our now two-year-old daughter from Ethiopia.

The summer of 2007, I traveled to Zambia with a team of adults and students who had been involved in this movement that only God could have orchestrated. This trip took place about five years after the Zambia Project started at Wheaton Academy. We had already raised half a million dollars toward World Vision's work in the Zamtan ADP, which was made up of nineteen thousand people living in three areas. I clearly remember a church service we had with the believers in Kakolo village during that trip. Although we shared little resemblance in looks, culture, speech, or living experiences, we entered into their daily life and circumstances and found community with them, just as Jesus entered into our physical world of uncertainty and unrest and provided us with eternal life. The Spirit of God brought unity as we all worshiped the same Lord. Through my tears during that service, I knew that God's purpose for me as a human being was to worship Him in Spirit and in truth. My heart began to open up and receive His love in its fullness.

Listen to me, dear brothers and sisters. Hasn't God chosen the poor in this world to be rich in faith? Aren't they the ones who will inherit the Kingdom he promised to those who love him? (James 2:5)[4]

That is the only way I can explain how I was drawn to begin the adoption process. My husband and I had been praying about starting a family of our own, but it no longer seemed to be about us and how we desperately wanted a child, but rather it was about following God's plan in creating a family of His choosing.

Here I am, four years later, teaching my Ethiopian daughter what it means to have compassion for the hurting, or even to simply share with those who don't have. She struggles, as do I, to make it less about the sacrifice in the moment, but instead to widen the scope to see that there are unlimited resources to be invested in and among God's children.

"The rich and poor have this in common: The LORD made them both" *(Proverbs 22:2)*[5]

I smile when I think of all the hills and valleys in my own journey to live out my Christian faith, and know that she too will have to experience the joy and the pain in living out her faith one day. Christ's work is manifesting itself daily. As His followers we choose to allow the Spirit to lead us. It is humbling to see that He can use us, if we are willing, to change the world through His transforming love. I wholeheartedly believe that we were meant to share in the journey of suffering others experience around us and live out the love that Jesus Christ embodied to a dying world. If you choose to believe and follow His lead, you'll never look back.

Martha taught math classes for sixteen years at Wheaton Academy where she also helped coach cross country and served as a faculty advisor for the Project LEAD team. She stopped teaching in 2009 so that she could stay home full time to care for her daughter Halle, adopted from Ethiopia. She and her husband, Steve, are currently waiting to adopt a little brother or sister for her from Africa.

CHAPTER 3

THE POWER OF STUDENT LEADERSHIP

I get all kinds of fascinating responses when people ask me what I do professionally. Most of them think being an educator is a very noble thing, but as they begin to ponder being with high school or college students for several hours every day they shake their heads and typically offer some sort of condolence for the pain I am enduring for the sake of bettering this generation of teenagers. They typically reply with phrases like "I could never do it. They would drive me nuts," or "You must have the patience of a saint to deal with all their immaturity."

The most humorous experiences typically take place in airports when I take larger groups of students on trips. I headed up a senior class trip to a dude ranch in Colorado for many years and when our group of one hundred or so high school seniors gathered at the boarding gate, the flight staff would begin to whisper and get flustered. They often offered a free of charge lecture about proper behavior before we even got on board. I have regularly been given an expletive-filled warning about what they think of teenagers when I announce that I am the guy in charge of this group. I graciously tell them to

please let me know if anything bad starts to happen and quietly tell
them that they really are a pretty great group of kids.

I've discovered over the last twenty years that students often garner little respect in our culture and are regularly viewed as being in
some sort of holding pattern where they are expected to just screw up
and play around before they somehow transition into being responsible adults.

Even as I've passed the age of forty, I still would often spend time
with high school or college students rather than people who are my
own age. Now perhaps part of it is that I haven't fully grown up, but
I'm not running around throwing toilet paper in trees or staying up
till 2 a.m. watching movies on weekend evenings. When even my
friends ask me why I haven't moved onto ministry with an older generation of people, I tell them stories of the joy I experience in seeing students do some pretty extraordinary things for the sake of the
Kingdom of God.

· One of the tenets I hold most deeply to in my theology is that
God is not concerned about chronological age when deciding whom
He chooses to accomplish His purposes in this world. I am convinced
that when Paul told Timothy to not let anyone look down on him just
because he was quite young to be in a leadership position, his words
are timeless and still need to be spoken to the younger members of
the body of Christ today. The Zambia Project story is an ongoing,
living testimony to the biblical reality that God is wanting and willing to use students as leaders and examples and Kingdom workers in
this and all other generations. I believed 1 Timothy 4:12 to be true
before we got involved with the issue of AIDS in Africa, but now I
am absolutely convinced that this verse must shape what we invite
and allow students to do as leaders and those on the front line of the
work of changing lives in dramatic and eternal ways.

I grew up as a high school and college student who naturally
slid into positions of leadership. As I served in leadership capacities

and both failed and excelled in those various roles, I developed a deep interest and belief in the power of leadership and the need for Christian churches and schools to cultivate the pursuit of seeking greater influence by today's students.

I read the Scriptures and saw God choose young people like Moses, Joseph, Samuel, David, Josiah, Daniel, Mary, Jesus, and Timothy as He anointed and appointed them as His leaders. They carried out His rule and reign in Israel and eventually all nations, and it was pretty clear that God was truly OK with people less than twenty-one years of age being in front rather than the back of the pack when it came to leadership. My look at church history, especially the last two hundred years or so, affirmed once again that students were often the leaders of God's great global revival movements as they together simply believed that His power would be made manifest in and through them as they prayed and spoke and acted in obedience to His commands. As I continued my work at Wheaton Academy I was often overwhelmed with the gifts and abilities and passions of the students sitting in and talking in my classrooms. I decided that one of the major focuses of my time and ministry at the school had to be in the development of a student leadership culture. We were ripe with candidates and we clearly saw our educational work having both a present and future impact on their lives and world.

I began a group called Project LEAD with the hope of equipping and empowering a group of senior students who would, through their leadership, exercise a powerful influence as examples and servants in our school community. It soon became one of the best parts of my job at Wheaton Academy. I saw up close the value of multiplying one's life out into another who will one day go on to do more than one person was capable of doing on his or her own. I even partnered with a local youth worker who started an organization called LeaderTreks that equipped hundreds of our students in incredibly effective and practical ways on nontraditional mission trip experiences.

Allow me to spend a few minutes explaining our intentional leadership development philosophy. At the Urbana Missions Conference in 1987 I picked up a classic text called *The Master Plan of Evangelism* by author and seminary professor Robert Coleman after hearing him speak at this missions event. In this book Coleman argues that we ought to read the Gospels and pay particular attention to the methods and strategies Jesus uses in His ministry and leadership development work. His thesis is that the very specific methods employed by Jesus in the first century are still the best ideas for how we are to be about God's Kingdom work in the twenty-first century. As I became more and more certain that the study of and execution of leadership was something I wanted to have as a central part of my own ministry career, I was particularly moved by Coleman's analysis of how Jesus prepared the disciples to be the leaders of the early church. These unlikely leaders would turn the world upside down, grow an organization over one hundred times in size in its first generation of existence, and still to this day be responsible for the creation of arguably the greatest body of influence in the world.

Here are a few pieces from *The Master Plan of Evangelism* that served as signposts in developing a leadership development program based on the life example of Jesus:

> *One cannot transform a world except as individuals in the world are transformed, and individuals cannot be changed except as they are molded in the hands of the Master. The necessity is apparent not only to select a few helpers but also to keep the group small enough to be able to work effectively with them.*

> *It also graphically illustrates a fundamental principle of teaching: that other things being equal, the more concentrated*

the size of the group being taught, the greater the opportunity for effective instruction.

Though Jesus did what he could to help the multitudes, he had to devote himself primarily to a few men, rather than the masses, so that the masses could at last be saved. Everything that is done with the few is for the salvation of the multitudes. This was the genius of his strategy.

We must decide where we want our ministry to count—in the momentary applause of popular recognition or in the reproduction of our lives in a few chosen people who will carry on our work after we have gone. Really it is a question of which generation we are living for.[6]

I am sure that many people who read this will quickly wonder, "Isn't this an exclusive way to do leadership development that leads to playing favorites? And what about all the other capable folks who don't make the special group of twelve?" These questions were asked and re-asked in my world. I would invite each member of the next senior class to apply for this student leadership team each winter and then only choose twelve (six senior guys, six senior girls) to be part of the team I worked with the following school year. It didn't seem to matter that I went to a model where the current members chose the team to avoid my own favoritism or bias, and that I communicated over and over again that this team was just one of many student leadership options at Wheaton Academy. I was often accused of being exclusive and not believing in the reality that everyone could be a leader. The attacks were often personal in nature toward me and I lost some really significant family and student relationships when a student wasn't chosen to be part of the next Project LEAD group.

More than once I was leaning toward doing away with the whole leadership team concept, but my students, the outcomes, and my rereading of the Gospels convinced me that I had to keep focusing on the few in terms of my own discipleship and leadership development so that we could effect change in the many within our school setting and the world beyond. Even after the success of the Zambia Project, this model, which had seemingly helped to produce change and impact on both the lives of those in the leadership team and the student body as a whole, was still often criticized and even vilified by students who didn't make the team, parents who were convinced their child was a great leader, and even fellow educators who didn't appreciate dealing with the negative vibe that is created when students don't make a team they have applied to be part of, especially when it isn't based just on athletic or academic credentials.

Ultimately, I believe that this intentional small team model of leadership development is the most effective one for a number of reasons. First, building and multiplying leaders happens on a small scale rather than a massive scale. I've been to hundreds of leadership events, but the sum of all I have heard and experienced at those events cannot compare in concrete leadership training impact to what I have learned from just a handful of key mentors. Their lives and shared experiences, questions and ideas, words of correction and encouragement, and prayers have truly shaped who I've become and the choices I have made in my personal and professional life. Creating life transformation in the realm of one's character requires consistent and authentic relational engagement.

Second, I have come to believe with all of my heart that the best leadership development is accomplished when growing leaders actually have to lead something. I know that sounds far too simplistic, but my experience has taught me with high school and college students that unless they feel the weight of being in charge of something significant they will *think* they can lead something, but may never move to that place where they *know* they can lead something.

Third, in order for us to get a community of students to be involved on a large-scale level, the student leadership team has to be crystal clear on the vision we are seeking to fulfill and then share it with their student peers. My experience has taught me that if we involve too many people in the creation and initial adoption of that vision, it becomes too diversified in thought and is not fully embraced by each member of the group who creates it. When this smaller group of leaders all has the chance to contribute in the development process, each voice is heard, and their affirmation is clear and strong concerning the end product, it makes the vision a powerful benchmark they believe in and will champion with deep conviction. And as they carry the vision to their peers, this deep personal belief and understanding causes them to pursue its mission with great passion and energy outside this smaller group!

Finally, the small group model of leadership allows for more effective accountability and evaluation. When you can look face-to-face and each person is familiar with what is going on in one another's lives and the way they are carrying out their specific responsibilities, it causes sharpening and greater productivity to naturally take place. Too often I have seen leaders go out from group meetings with a vision of what they are going to do, but they end up hiding and never being challenged about what could actually take place because there is not the clear and healthy follow-up that we all need in the process of seeking to make a big and compelling vision become reality.

The Zambia Project is without a doubt a story about student leadership in the twenty-first century. My relationships and work with hundreds of student leaders over the past twenty years have been the highlight and the challenge of my work as a campus pastor and educator. I would never trade this part of my job and my life for any other type of ministry experience. For so many years I believed in my head that students could be and should be leaders and now I know in my heart that a bunch of high school or college kids can change the world. This movement of God on our campus was envisioned and structured and carried through to completion by a bunch of students. They were inspired first and foremost by a group of senior student leaders year after year who brought about sweeping cultural change as leaders in truly remarkable and unprecedented ways. I watched it happen and often stood back with great surprise at what my little tribe of very normal American students could do when they were allowed to lead and to speak to their peers about responding to the greatest needs of our world today.

I took on the roles of shepherding, advocating, praying, questioning, and cheerleading very often over the last ten years, but I often deferred the role of actual hands-on leadership to the students whom I was teaching and discipling. They didn't shy away from the leadership roles and costs, but embraced them and exerted influence in ways I simply could not as a teacher and administrator on our campus.

As I preach the gospel of the power of student leadership to my church and education leader friends, they often look at me with a face that features their mouth in a small smirk and eyes that display doubt. After I respond to their look and initial skepticism, they ultimately say something like, "I've heard all about student leadership and it looks great on paper, but I still need to be convinced that when push comes to shove, it is actually viable and worth all the potential trouble it could bring me." Their hidden thoughts, which they won't voice until later on in the discussion, basically state that they have spent a lot of time looking for and hiring competent and gifted adults who are paid to create curriculums and programs that will educate and change student lives. They are simply not certain that students can do anything that would trump the job the adults can do. They know it will happen without as many mistakes if an adult does it and are aware of the reality that students will need more guidance and supervision and chunks of their time than a professional will need in doing the same type of leadership work.

All these kinds of thoughts are logical and are sensible if you compare the intellectual and administrative capabilities of adults versus students in determining who should be in leadership positions and hold the real power in a school or church context. So in light of these questions, why would I write a book that offers this different model? Because I believe it will bring about transformational change in student lives and greater participation in a community project that will dramatically alter for the better the spiritual climate in your institution or group. Let me add a few thoughts that flow directly out of my personal experience and I believe reflect God's belief in the capacity of His student disciples and His unique gifting for those who are young in age to play very key roles in what He can do through His servants in our world today.

First, a student who embraces God's vision does it with a level of personal commitment and buy-in that is nothing less than all-out in terms of participation. I have watched students hear about the needs of people in sub-Saharan Africa, and then they simply respond. They don't consider all the questions of what if the economy goes bad, what if the funds I give don't do exactly what I think they should, or what if I will need these resources for something else down the road in my life. They don't have all the preconceptions and cultural biases toward African people and development work that many adults carry around with them. As God has stirred in them a heart for the poor, they have made a simple decision that the scope of their need demands that same scope of response. I've gone to the bank with a senior guy to help him withdraw so much money out of his account at the bank to help build a school building that the teller spent several minutes grilling us on the wisdom of this choice, almost refusing to make out the check to World Vision. I've had a group of a dozen kids take the lead and personally make pledges and then follow through with gifts of

over $10,000 towards the building of a new medical facility through
their own work, sacrifices, and generous giving. What so many would
call the naivety of youth has caused them to be the kind of authentic
and confident leaders whose faith overcomes fear and whose belief
in their cause overwhelms questions and opposition that arise. They
were and continue to be the kind of disciples who at face value decide
to do what Scripture commands us to do and what their heart com-
pels them to respond to in both word and deed.

Second, in trying to create a project that would capture the imagination of our student community, there simply was and is no better
way to have students join the team than if they are recruited by those
who are just like them. As students were the central voice and the
designers and implementers of our project initiatives and fundraisers, their peers saw them do things that they then believed they could
do as well. Almost all of our myriad of activities and strategies to
raise resources for our community in Zambia were created and run
from start to finish by students themselves. There was a clear understanding established in our school community that each and every
student was welcome to come up with and then execute their own
ideas without needing to have adults in positions of leadership overly
involved. We asked that they inform us of what their latest ideas were,
but we rarely said no and they went far beyond our expectations in
the creativity and results produced as they owned the execution of
the vision of this project. It became fashionable and quite valued
to be one of those who would host the latest Zambia Project fundraiser, and the positive peer pressure to do things on behalf of the
poor somewhere along the line became a pretty unstoppable force
for good in our student culture. I've watched hundreds and hundreds
of students lead everything from a simple bake sale at lunch to large
community events such as 5K runs and elaborate auctions. Standing
in the background of most of these events I have been convinced
of that which Scripture affirms throughout its entirety: God is no

respecter of age when it comes to anointing those whom He wants to do His Kingdom work!

In a very strange way, I've seen a connection between the belief in the gifts and leadership abilities of high school students and their belief in the dignity, value, and potential of the children of Zambia. There is a cultural system in both settings that devalues at times the importance of their role in the larger society. Students are incredibly privileged and even spoiled in our American context, but they are often not expected to be able to make any significant contribution to the bettering of humanity and the world till they are done with the ever lengthening years of discovering their identity and finding themselves and their place in the world. They are gripped by entertainment options and given little formal responsibility outside of academic workloads. In the African culture, children are often completely denied the opportunity to grow and learn and thrive as they receive smaller food portions and limited medical help while being forced to quit school to work in agricultural roles or serve as surrogate parents to younger siblings. Some of this is clearly done out of necessity, but some of it is also done due to a worldview that does not value their place in an adult male dominated community.

The Zambia Project has not only caused many of our students to fall in love with the children of Africa, but it has elevated their status as ministers in God's Kingdom work so that they can then lift up the value of children in Africa and provide hope and dreams for a very different future. I love that the belief in the potential of the poorest of the poor by a group of adolescents here in America can directly serve to change the life vision of children in Zambia. It is now conceivable that they can escape the poverty and disease and despair found in a life that does not reflect what God has intended them to experience on this planet. I continue to revel in and be humbled by the matching hand of the God of the universe. He longs to use those whom are least expected to do that which He is most anxious to do as He connects

His people together in relationship that changes the future trajectory and belief system of both of their lives.

In many ways, I continue to daily stake my very life and ministry on this foundational notion that God is interested in creating divine moments and movements through the service and passion and ideas of those who are the youngest in His church. I will continue to push and even be a bit overbearing and obnoxious about giving students and young adults places of prominence and power in the growth and leadership of the body of Christ in the years to come, even as I get further removed from their age and worlds. I will do so because as I sit in meetings with my colleagues where we think and converse and debate that latest program or budget issues, I hear in my head voices of a generation of students who regularly scream at me that they want to do something. They want to bring change to people's lives in this very day and time. And when the Holy Spirit has clearly led them to step out in faith to do something magnificent on God's behalf, I will continue to try to clear the way of all that would distract and keep them from moving forward as they lead from a place of unbridled trust that God will show up in their lives. That is indeed the summary of the story God has written at Wheaton Academy because His students have "walked by faith and not by sight" over and over again.

HALLELUJAH! HALLELUJAH!

Jenell Giannini

Click. One click of a mouse and I am back—back in a land over nine thousand miles away—back in Africa. I had selected the picture folder entitled "Africa Love." I am not sure what I meant when I titled that folder almost five months ago, but today, right now, it means that I love Leviticus. One click of a mouse on the picture folder entitled "Family Time: Graduation Party" and memories begin to stir—warm, welcoming memories. The pictures in this folder were taken the same summer I traveled to Africa. As I scroll through these frozen memories, I cannot help but notice Alexa, my little cousin. She is older than Leviticus—maybe two or three years. I cannot remember taking as many pictures of her as my picture file suggests I had. I can assume that she managed to coax her sister into producing a mini photo shoot with herself as the primary model, something Leviticus wouldn't have even thought to do. These two young children have shaped my life. Leviticus, the little boy whom I have met once, and Alexa, the little girl who has my face structure and mannerisms.

Click. My first interaction with Leviticus was in the Commons of Wheaton Academy, my former high school. We were hosting what is known as the "World Vision Aids Experience." This event helped people understand what it would be like to live in an African village, wondering if they were HIV positive or not. Each person assumed the role of an African child as a means of understanding the hardships these children face daily. At the end of each person's journey, he or she would find a prayer room for reflection, a story room for education, and a room filled with pictures of African children, with eyes pleading for action. At the end of my journey I managed to make eye contact with a child. His eyes pierced the page with sadness. His lips curled slightly downwards, forming a small frown. His picture begged for my acknowledgment. After staring into the eyes of this small child for several minutes, I decided that I wanted to know more, maybe even to become a part of his life. So, I requested to sponsor Leviticus, and I took his picture home with me.

The day I made the commitment to sponsor little Leviticus was quite significant. I had just agreed to travel to Zambia, and being in that AIDS exhibit had jolted my emotions. I had been waiting for my opportunity to travel to Africa for two years, and the day that my desire would become my experience was quickly approaching. I was in a mock African environment holding a mere image of a child, but one day soon I would be in real Africa, holding a living, breathing child in my arms. Leviticus was my closest connection to Africa, and I was so excited to be a part of even the smallest facets of his life.

Click. I cannot even remember the first time I held little Alexa in my arms. I was twelve years old when she was born. She is six years old now, her sister only two years her senior. Alexa is the baby of the family, and I am the oldest grandchild. She has my same, thick hair—the only difference being that hers is much darker than my strawberry blonde coloring. She has the same round face that I do, and the same blue eyes. She is tall though, much taller than I ever was as a child. Grandma and Grandpa like to spoil little Alexa. They like to spoil all of us, but Alexa has a special charm that the rest of us seem to lack. As I look through her pictures, even I cannot help but be charmed by this spirited girl. Alexa and I may share the same eye color, but hers are bigger and brighter. Her smirk is a bit devious, although terribly cute—even with the little gap between her two front teeth (something I had until I was ten). I have plenty of snapshots of those brilliant eyes and that sly smile.

One of the many snapshots is of Alexa, her sister, and my other cousin, Johnny. They are all blowing bubbles with Aunt Jules. I acted as the photographer and captured my unknowing subjects in their bliss. In this shot, each person is eagerly blowing bubbles as if it was their life's work. Alexa, however, is sitting close to my aunt—posing for my *intended* candid photo. Her grin is poised and coy. I cannot help but chuckle as I think back to this scene. My aunt was assigned to watch the kids; she was doing a fantastic job at keeping them out of everyone's way. They were having so much fun as they blew bubbles, played board games, ate cookies, and basked in the affection of their adoring family. It seemed that life could not have gotten any sweeter for Alexa and her companions. This memory is precious. After looking through an entire album of my family celebrating my high school graduation with me, I cannot help but think of the people in Africa—little Leviticus.

Click. I'm back in the "Africa Love" folder. My cursor automatically slides to the pictures of Leviticus. I had taken these photos while I was in Africa. I was privileged to meet Leviticus, visit his home, pray for his family, and tell him that I love him. That little boy who I sometimes saw as just a picture taped to my wall became human and tangible. Those same sad eyes pierced me once again. That same small frown challenged me. I was drawn to him. And sadly, I almost missed my chance.

Several months before we left for Africa, we were told that those on the trip who sponsor children living in Kakolo Village would get the opportunity of a lifetime: they would be able to meet those precious children. Leviticus did not live in Kakolo Village. I was supposed to relay his name to the trip leaders just in case we stopped in another village, even though it was not on the itinerary. I didn't even want to bother—I didn't want to feel the sting of disappointment if I was in his country, maybe even just miles away, and never got to meet him. I fought that fear of potential disappointment and at the last possible minute, I informed World Vision of the relationship Leviticus and I shared. Several weeks later, as I sat on the plane bound for Africa, I opened my itinerary. The only other village we were headed for was Kapaluwe: the home of Leviticus and his family. My jaw slightly dropped. I felt like running up and down the aisles screaming "Hallelujah! Hallelujah!" (But I am pretty sure the other passengers would not have appreciated this boisterous celebration.) Even though I did not physically display my overwhelming joy, I was no less thrilled to meet the child who inspired me to live a less selfish, more sacrificial life.

I couldn't help but set the picture of Leviticus, my sponsored child, and Alexa, my cousin, side by side. These pictures represent people—people whom I love, who challenge me. Alexa inspires me, but not in the way Leviticus does. Alexa asks me questions—she wants to know about the world and how it works. Her inquisitive nature forces me to think critically about the seemingly normal quirks of life. When she asks me why the stars only come out at night, I must attempt to explain God's creativity. When she asks me why I call my father "Daddy" and why she calls my father "Uncle Remo," I must attempt to explain family connections. These types of questions inspire me to appreciate ordinary blessings such as the brilliant glow of stars in the night and a family who dearly loves me.

Leviticus sleeps under those same stars. He too has a loving family. A part of me would like to dwell on those blessings that Alexa, Leviticus, and I share. But it's impossible to do so after having stood in Leviticus' home. He lives in a tiny hut with his parents, grandmother, and little sister, Loveness. He eats his meals while sitting on the floor of this hut. There is no room for a table, or even a single bed. The hut contains two couches. One serves as a closet, kitchen cabinet, and a bookshelf—all of their personal possessions are piled on this piece of furniture. The other is for sitting, maybe sleeping. Their bathroom is a hole in the ground directly to the left of their hut. Their stove is a fire pit directly to the right. Their roof has holes in it, making any unfortunate weather disastrous.

Alexa is growing up in one of the wealthiest suburbs of Illinois. She attends a private Montessori school. Her home has five bedrooms—she has her own room. She has a walk-in closet. She chooses her own outfit to wear every morning from the wide collection of clothes that fill this walk-in closet. She has a swimming pool in her backyard. Her daddy has three cars, one of which is a Corvette. She has a college fund set aside for years in the future. If she got sick, she would have a variety of doctors at her disposal.

Leviticus and his family cannot comprehend this kind of excess and abundance. Before I was brought to Leviticus's home, I was introduced to him on the sidelines of a "futbol" game. His nose was running and his eyes were glossy from crying. I handed him a big stuffed animal—it was a heffa-lump from *Pooh's Heffalump Movie*. Leviticus burst into tears—I had scared him with my oversized American toy. In attempts to quiet his screams of anx-iety, I pulled out two green Hot Wheels toy cars. He looked at me, paused, then looked at the cars and slowly plucked them from my hand. His tears eventually stopped trickling down his face, but a smile never crossed his lips. It was then that his mother told me he was sick. When she said "sick" I assumed she meant "cold" or "cough" or "flu."

Later that day as I sat on that little couch in Leviticus's hut, I asked his mom questions about her life. I learned that her husband was a farmer who has little work to do right now. I learned that this mother of two recently began attending school for the first time in her life. I was most troubled by this conversation when I learned that Leviticus was very sick. His mother had taken him to the nearby medical clinic and was given malaria pills. She was told that he may not have malaria, but for preventative purposes he should take the medication. *"Malaria!"* I felt like screaming. How could this sweet boy have malaria? It just didn't seem possible. I still do not know if he has that awful disease, but even the possibility is horrendous enough.

Even though this meeting crushed my spirit, I can still remember that day with a fondness for the beauty of Leviticus and his family. While I was in his hut, his mother opened a tattered old Bible and removed three pictures—one of her husband, one of Loveness, and one of Leviticus. The World Vision staff had taken the two pictures of her children—the one of Leviticus was the same one I was given upon my sponsorship. That Bible seemed to hold the only things of real value to her. When she held out the picture of Leviticus for me to see, I couldn't help looking back and forth between the beautiful child before me and the picture that brought his mother hope.

Snap. I vividly remember Alexa posing naturally for the camera every time her sister prepared to take a snapshot of her. She stood in front of the camera with confidence. She smiled and laughed. Leviticus could only stare straight ahead into the lens of the camera. No smile, no laughter, just a child scarred by poverty. I long for the day Leviticus smiles for the camera.

If someone were to browse through my picture files they would find images reflecting the middle-class American lifestyle as well as the average-impoverished African lifestyle. But it's not about what Alexa has and what Leviticus doesn't have. They are both children; they have just been brought up in two different cultures. They will both grow up and have dreams; they both already have dreams. Those dreams, whatever they may be, bring me hope.

I remember being asked when I was their age, "What do you want to be when you grow up?" I assume Alexa is asked the same question, and I wonder if Leviticus will ever be asked this question. Now that I am older, others have stopped asking me, but I still ask myself. The day I connected with Leviticus's big eyes, I knew the answer would always be, "lover of people."

Meeting Leviticus made poverty a personal issue—I cannot live as if his problems have nothing to do with me. Those problems are my problems. I send a check once a month to help relieve some of the financial burden that Leviticus's family has, but that isn't enough. So I pray. I pray that Leviticus will be properly diagnosed and cured. I pray that his father's crops will be bountiful. I pray that his mother's education will help insure a second income. I pray that Loveness will grow to become a healthy, happy little girl. And I pray that I will see Leviticus again—only this time, with a big, brilliant smile on his face.

Jenell is finishing her studies at Indiana Wesleyan University as an English Education major. She has recently accepted a job with Teach For America, and will be part of the 2012 Chicago corps.

CHAPTER 4

THE MOVEMENT OF THE HOLY SPIRIT

Sometimes as the "leader" of this project, I am almost embarrassed to admit that I didn't draw up or help my students create a "business plan" that I would have been able to show potential donors and critics alike. When I take a look back at our project and try to identify specifically how this rather large chunk of resources was gathered, there simply isn't a brilliant marketing model or strategic plan that served as the guiding framework leading us to the achievement of our long-term goals. In many ways, this thing we experienced called the Zambia Project doesn't easily fit into a normal framework or program model.

When you begin to talk about a sustained financial movement that is responsible for raising several hundred thousand dollars, certain leadership and fundraising assumptions are usually made. Most philanthropy experts would assume this project was heavily led by aggressive and networked adults who got some rather significant donors to respond to a very compelling need in sub-Saharan Africa. In fact, the organization that we partnered with in this venture, World Vision, is the largest Christian non-governmental organization in the world through implementation of this strategy in a brilliant and systematic way all over the world. However, the only single "master strategy" we truly relied on was a belief in the power and activity of the Holy Spirit in the lives of our students and the people of the world where God's Kingdom activity showed up time and time again.

In my own faith journey, the role of the Holy Spirit has been ignored, misunderstood, and basically relegated to a very secondary place in both the development of my theology and the living out of my faith as a Christian. Many of my friends here in the States and especially overseas have held a much higher view of the role of the Holy Spirit in life, worship, and activity in the world. This difference has often caused me to question if my faith was too much aligned with and structured upon what I could logically explain, managerially control, and confidently accomplish through human initiative and skill. I have been and continue to be so much more comfortable developing well-crafted mission and vision statements that help me diagram on paper with conviction and certainty how we can and will do some really cool and really big things on God's behalf.

I am a huge proponent of helping everyone figure out how they are internally wired and discover their spiritual gifts to be most effective as participants in the gospel work Scripture invites us to do each day with our lives. I have given many of my Spiritual Leadership classes and student leadership teams detailed personality and spiritual gifts inventories because I believe that when they discover who they are and how God has gifted them they can then be released to specific and intentional places of service in the body of Christ. I have even given hundreds of students and adults over the last several years the StrengthsFinder Inventory from the Gallup folks before making charts with the spots where they can do the most good in seeking to make a difference in the world. In fact, the first group of students who birthed this project would tell you that knowing and accepting and acting upon their strengths brought wonderful chemistry and competence to their group's decisions on what to do as they tried to raise the initial money needed to construct the Kakolo Village schoolhouse.

However, if I am honest, students who have not graduated from high school most often are not yet able to do exactly what professional fundraisers have been trained to do, and they frankly don't have the mind-set or patience to build a foolproof economic development model that will help raise out of poverty and disease an AIDS-devastated community on the other side of the world.

The bottom line is that from a human perspective, it makes absolutely no sense that this community of teenagers would have the thinking ability, giftedness, and creative genius to pull off a six-year grassroots project that would raise over $100,000 a year for the poorest of the poor in a country almost everyone around them couldn't even begin to place on a world map. But then I read anew a passage with the moving words of Paul in Ephesians 3:16, 20:

> *I pray that out of his glorious riches he may strengthen you with power through his Spirit in your inner being.... Now to him who is able to do immeasurably more than all we ask or imagine, according to his power that is at work within us.*[7]

Having done some reading about the global history of the church in a seminary class, I guess I probably shouldn't have been surprised to see God's Spirit sweep through a group of young people causing spiritual revival and response taking place in their hearts that transformed how they chose to live. Here are just a few examples from history of the work of God's Spirit:

> In 1729 John and Charles Wesley, along with other students formed the "Holy Club" at Oxford University. This was the beginning of the Methodist Church and a dynamic preaching and discipleship ministry in both Europe and North America.

The Haystack Prayer Meeting, led by Samuel John Mills at Williams College in Massachusetts in 1806, is viewed by many scholars as the seminal event for the development of Protestant missions in the subsequent decades and centuries, and a key part of the Second Great Awakening.

The Student Volunteer Movement in the late nineteenth century spurred over six thousand college students to go into overseas missions service in places like China and other parts of Africa and Asia.

Campus organizations like InterVarsity Christian Fellowship and Campus Crusade, along with the Urbana Missions Conference of the twentieth century have seen millions of students become Christ followers and engaged in ministry all over the globe.

Poverty and social justice movements like the ONE Campaign, Micah Challenge, Tearfund, and International Justice Mission have attracted millions of young Christians who have responded to meet the immense physical needs and injustices present in our world today.

Another foundational biblical truth we saw become reality was the simple truth that the Spirit of God would take our prayers and our passions before the Father, and He would answer with the movement of His Spirit far exceeding the faith and requests of our prayers.

In our first year trying to get the vision accepted and the student body on board, we got to a place about three or four months into the start-up of the project where we found ourselves out of fresh ideas and ways to make it easy for their peers to get involved. We had tried several different types of fundraising events and had even published a list of Top 10 Ways to Get Involved in the Zambia Project that we handed out to each student on our campus. Yet as we sat in the school library eating pizza one night taking stock of where we were, we discovered we had raised about $5000, less than 10 percent of our goal for the year, and we had just over two months before this team of senior leaders were scheduled to graduate. At the current rate of participation and giving, we would finish well over $40,000 short of being able to fund the building of this schoolhouse we so decisively believed God had called us to see built in this community that now knew we were planning on providing for them.

I remember setting up another brainstorming session when the other teacher and partner in our Project LEAD initiative, as well as one of the most godly and deeply centered followers of Jesus I knew, spoke up. She asked a simple question to every single one of us sitting in frustration around the table, "Have you guys been praying for this project every day?" No one spoke back in reply, but the silence clearly communicated our answer, and at that moment the Spirit of God spoke to our hearts and said this is indeed the strategy we hadn't trusted or tried yet in seeking to do this Kingdom work.

So we did what any thinking person in that moment would have done. We decided to ask God to send His Spirit and move in the hearts of students to raise this money that our best ideas and programs and presentations couldn't seem to produce. We covenanted with each other as a team that every day we would ask God to continue to stir in our student body and we would plead with God to specifically have them give, even if it didn't involve a campaign or activity or new idea that would grab and hold their attention. In fact, this group of students even began to fast, skipping a lunch or two each week, meeting in my small office to pray together that God would do what we believed He wanted to do in the first place. A funny thing happened: God heard our cries and released His Spirit in an unusual way in an unusual place, a high school campus full of American teenagers.

Since the days of Pentecost, has the whole church ever put aside every other work and waited upon Him for ten days, that the Spirit's power might be manifested? We give too much attention to method and machinery and resources, and too little to the source of power.
Jeremy Taylor, seventeenth century British pastor and theologian[8]

A couple of senior guys had built a small replica of the schoolhouse we were hoping to see built in Zambia, painted the words "Zambia Project" on it, and placed it in the back of the commons room where students ate their lunches every day. They had carved out a little hole in the top of the schoolhouse where students could anonymously slide in gifts of support for the project. We began after spring break a daily ritual of unlocking that schoolhouse lid and gathering up the money dropped into the box on that particular day. In many ways, it was such a strange thing. We were expecting God to provide money at Wheaton Academy almost like He did daily manna for the Israelites that could be used to meet the daily need for education in the Kakolo Village community in Zambia.

And to our astonishment and as a remarkable answer to our prayers, just like He did in the wilderness of the desert in Moses' day, He showed up and provided just what we needed. The Holy Spirit who lived inside so many of our students invited and convinced them to give, to give in sacrificial and generous ways. Many days we would walk the hundred yards or so from the lunchroom to my office with our arms full of one-, five-, ten-, and twenty-dollar bills that were stuffed into the little hole in this grey box.

These daily money-counting sessions became times when we often felt like we were standing on holy ground and experiencing truly the presence of God Almighty as He had moved in ways we couldn't understand or begin to imagine. I remember that day in early May when the number on my little calculator told me that we had now passed the magic number of $53,000 identified in a catalog as the price tag for the new school several months ago. Tears came down my face and the faces of some of my students while we also whooped and hollered a little bit, surely interrupting another teacher's lecture to students across the hallway. As I thought back on how this amount of money had come in I quickly realized that I didn't actually know how it had happened. Many, many anonymous donations from students ages fourteen to eighteen were dropped in a box with the trust that God would change other kids' lives with their gifts, and the Spirit of God had provoked them to respond to the needs of people they had only seen once or twice represented in a picture projected on a screen.

At our next meeting, we got down in reverence and we prayed and acknowledged the power of God's Spirit to do that which we could not do ourselves and that which He had planned to do all along: to expand the faith of a group of young followers of Jesus and bring healing and hope to the children He loved so very much in a little village in Africa. In many ways, this unexplainable response changed my life, my faith, and my view of God and His children forever.

Over a six-week period in the spring of 2003, a community of five hundred students gave over $70,000 in cash to respond to the global AIDS pandemic and the Holy Spirit became very real in a fresh and compelling way I had never seen before in all my years of knowing and following Christ. And while we marveled at God's Spirit moving hearts to care and give in obedience to the call of God here in Chicago, the Spirit of God stirred in Zambia in a remarkable way as well. When told that their new school had been fully funded by these strangers from America, the people of Kakolo Village fell to their knees before God and spent two days thanking Him and praying for the needs of Wheaton Academy students as their offering back to the God who had answered their prayers in a dramatic way. God's Spirit was on the move, literally across the globe, showing up in truly remarkable ways.

When many people first hear this story they tend to wonder most about how we were able to create the initial momentum that could get a vision that seemed a bit outrageous to eventually become so strong that it grew exponentially and continues to live on in the Wheaton Academy school community today. In doing some analysis trying to discover the reason for why our vision became so deeply rooted, a few simple principles Andy Stanley talks about in his book *Visioneering* proved to be true in our experience. Many times we find ourselves with a dream about something big we believe we can and should do to change the world and make a difference in people's lives. Yet that initial vision often is not sustained or even brought to a public announcement despite people's great initial interest and very real passion to be a part of something significant. I had actually been a part of tens if not hundreds of conversations with students over the previous decade where they had expressed great enthusiasm for a particular idea and then it was long gone within the next thirty days. They rarely would come back with another grand idea because they began to believe that it was probably pointless to try to make big stuff happen in the first place.

Here is a summary of thoughts that went from excerpts of Spiritual Leadership class assignments on Andy Stanley's book to team mantras. We saw these lived out in God's remarkable timing as the Holy Spirit moved as we believed and acted in faith in response to our vision:

A Vision Is Born:

Our vision was born in our souls where we became consumed with the vast difference between what is and what could be.

We were deeply dissatisfied with both seeing and living out the status quo in our lives, and the chance to respond as evangelical Christians in a tangible way to the global AIDS pandemic became not just merely something we hoped could be done, but it became something that must be done.

Our calling to be part of God's Kingdom response in Africa was no longer a good idea, but a God idea. This God-ordained vision became a moral imperative.

This seemingly God-given and ordained vision truly lined up with what God seemed to be up to in the world. There seemed to be this almost divine correlation between what was happening in a few students' hearts and what He was up to in awakening the American evangelical church at almost the very same moment in time.

The God of How:

Andy Stanley simply states this important principle: what always precedes how. He claims that very often we will know what God has put in our hearts to do long before we know how He intends to bring it about.

How is not a problem for God! Divine visions require divine intervention, as Stanley reminds us in this sentence, "What God originates, God orchestrates."

A final summary of these principles is that there are both good ideas and God ideas that we entertain as followers of Jesus. God ideas aren't limited because of the resources possessed by the God of the universe; we in many ways stand back and watch it happen.[9]

"I myself do nothing. The Holy Spirit accomplishes all through me."
William Blake, eighteenth and nineteenth century English poet
and philosopher[10]

In the whole of the Zambia Project story, the biggest key for us
was locking in on what it was He had called us to do. The *what* was
crystal clear and we couldn't afford to abandon the vision or see it not
get done because it was a matter of life and death, and it reflected the
very heart and passions of the One we worshipped and took all direction from in our lives. As the *what* became central to our lives, our
minds, and our hearts, God then orchestrated this remarkable series
of events in such a way that just about everyone involved recognized
the big and beautiful thumbprint of God in all that was done.

I really do believe we felt a sense of what the early church in Acts
2 and 4 felt as God moved in and through their midst in the first
century. We read and tried to apply the truth of these remarkable
verses. They model best a group of Jesus followers who believed in
the reality, power, and work of the Holy Spirit promised days before
by Jesus himself as they simply did the work of caring for the needs
of all people and telling people they were doing it because of a Savior
who had died on behalf of them.

*Everyone was filled with awe at the many wonders and signs
performed by the apostles....God's grace was so powerfully at
work in them all. (Acts 2:43, 4:33)[11]*

One of our biggest cheerleaders and encouragers in this journey
of responding to the needs of the poor has been Steve Haas, Chief
Catalyst at World Vision USA, who is one of the most articulate and
compelling voices on behalf of the poor in our world today. Several
years ago over coffee Steve looked at me and said something that
brilliantly encapsulated what had happened in the midst of God's use

of students in chasing this divine vision. He said, "Chip, what you've done is simply released these kids to do that which God wanted to do with them all along." This notion that we would trust God enough to release students to be the leaders of things adults were only supposed to be capable of doing was not and still is not the easiest of things to do. In fact, I think it only really happened because we believed the power of the Holy Spirit was way bigger than the realities of age or experience or competence that seemed to argue for limiting and managing student initiatives (the more typical paradigm in student ministry and work) rather than the more radical concepts of freedom and release when it comes to big visions and "little" people.

In the early days of our project I think the decision to actually let a group of students passionately go public with a vision to take on the world's biggest health crisis and try to make an actual dent in its spread and impact was seen as either cute or somewhat reckless by those around me. I think many of our parents and my professional colleagues thought it might be unwise to set these teenagers up for failure in attempting to achieve a very public goal that was probably too big for them to accomplish. Our ministry partner, World Vision, was excited about seeing young people with such a passion for the very issues their organization cared most about, but even they had made contact with a large donor who could make up the rather sizable monetary difference they expected would exist after the students' fundraising efforts were complete. They wanted the schoolhouse project to be finished and for the students at Wheaton Academy to feel a sense of completion even though they had fallen short of their big dream.

Obviously, God had different thoughts when it came to the notion of unleashing students to teach and surprise those around them who doubted what they could do to truly change the world. This generation and this particular community of students continues to hold on to a distinct longing and need to make a difference with their lives.

And they want this difference to be tangible, to improve the conditions and future for real people's lives, and for their own gifts and resources to be used to reflect the values and vision of the One who came to bring life in all its fullness (John 10:10) to all people in every place on the planet He created. They are not content to wait for this to take place when they are fully educated and fully trained; they want to see hope and a better future invade the lives of people right now in answer to their desperate cries and prayers for help.

As we have watched this growing passion for justice and compassionate care growing in the hearts and minds of a student generation, we who are mentoring and teaching them can do one of two things. We can tell them to wait and essentially set up hidden roadblocks that turn them back around into their own lives that can be void of significance beyond the latest toy or romance or noticeable achievement. Or, we can say, "It is risky and uncertain and will most likely be messy, but we have to drop the gate and release them to action and responsibility. Our faith is in the power of the One who resides in them and can empower them to do that which they want to see happen with their lives." We saw the collision of the adult release of students to dream big and act on their visions with their own internal desires to be difference makers and culture changers do something dramatic in our little Christian school. The collision was felt by our students in West Chicago, Illinois and the children of Kakolo Village, Zambia, and the Spirit's power shook the foundation of both communities.

In the earliest days of this faith adventure, the first group of student leaders watched what I would definitely name as one of my top five favorite movies of all times. *Field of Dreams* is a somewhat sappy, mystical film about a middle-aged man who builds a baseball field in the middle of a cornfield in Iowa because he hears a mysterious voice whisper several times to him, "If you build it, he will come."[12] I fell in love with the movie when I first saw it because of the intersection of an outrageous dream, baseball heroes, and the main character's relationship with his dad. Throughout the movie, the main character in the film, Ray Kinsella, is told by everyone from his wife, brother-in-law, neighbors, and his own doubts that to follow this leading, this voice, to build a beautiful baseball field on his land where his major crop sits is, as a farmer, absolutely crazy at its best, and delusional at its worst. Yet that calling is strong enough to see Kinsella through unexplained trips to Fenway Park and northern Minnesota, the laughter of his peers, and all kinds of hidden questions and fears as he works to construct the kind of field he always dreamed of playing on as a young child who was the son of a minor league catcher. By the end of the film, not only have former great baseball stars come out of the corn to play baseball games one more time, but Kinsella's estranged father finally appears and the two of them "have a catch," and that which Ray always dreamed would happen becomes reality. When he builds the field, the person who matters most to him in his life does indeed come.

In the strangest of ways, this older movie became the chosen metaphor for our own journey to build a schoolhouse and create permanent life change for the children of Zambia. For almost a decade there was a T-shirt hanging in my office with the motto written in marker across the back, "If we build it, they will come." Early on in the project I got an e-mail with a simple picture of this group of smiling African children standing in an overgrown field where the first school ever in their community was to be built. Their expressions and faces screamed at me that their future depended in some way on my own personal faith and trust in the voice of God that I heard whispering in my ear to do that which seemed unpopular, undoable, and unexplainable at the time and place where I found myself. The still, small voice of God that was often threatened to be drowned out by other's opinions and other needs and interests was clear enough, loud enough, and compelling enough to cause a small group of His young followers to join Him in creating their own field of dreams in a place they could only imagine in their minds. The Holy Spirit still speaks today to those who know the One who promised that He would send Him in all power and clarity and force to a world where so, so many were and are desperate for a taste of the divine, for food to eat, water to drink, and a place to be healed and to learn. May the Spirit of God that is present in downtown Chicago, the beaches of west Michigan, the cornfields of Iowa, and the dusty trails and villages of Zambia continue to be trusted, embraced, and released as we invite Him to invade our world and do that which we could only dream about before He came upon the scene.

REFLECTION

WHO IS THIS GOD?

Tony Frank

My name is Tony Frank and I am a major gifts fundraiser for World Vision based in Chicago. In this role, I have the privilege of representing the organization to individuals who wish to fund our work around the globe. Typically this means that I meet with people who are able to make significant gifts, and I share with them about our work while inviting them to partner with us. It was during my first few months on the job that I received a call from a colleague at our headquarters who told me about high school students who were raising funds to build a school in Zambia. Since they were located in my area, I went to meet with their leader, Chip Huber, because I wanted to learn more about their story. Now you have to understand that this was a bit of a stretch for me, as they didn't fit the typical profile of a donor that I would normally call upon. But I was new, anxious to build connections, and I also had a heart for young people. I distinctly recall thinking on the way to the meeting that their rather large goal was admirable, but I actually felt they would be doing well if they raised around $10,000.

Boy was I wrong. Not only that, but I also underestimated what God was about to do on their campus through this group of committed young people. I had no idea. Who is this God who calls us to take steps of faith on behalf of others, and who allows us to be a part of His response to the needs of the world? And why does He choose to bless us along the way?

In the days that followed my meeting with Chip, I was humbled as I saw how students began sacrificing on behalf of others whom they might never meet. As the end of the school year approached, a flurry of support brought in the funds for the construction of the school. Not only that amount, but more had been raised than was needed. I was amazed by what God had done through this group of students.

I thought they would call it a great success, and then move on. But they decided to keep up the work in the Zambian community and try again the next year. This time I thought for sure that the second year would prove the first year to be a one-time special experience. And again I was wrong, and I was humbled by this God who continued to refuse to fit into the box I had arranged for Him.

This pattern has been replayed throughout my experience in working with Wheaton Academy: take a step of faith, see God move, and marvel at who He is. In the process of thinking that I am helping someone else, I end up being the one helped. My faith has stretched and been strengthened, and I've grown in my relationship with others and with the One who is behind it all.

In his book *Walking with the Poor*, author Bryant Myers points out that the nature of poverty is relational. Poverty is a result of relationships that do not work; relationships with ourselves, each other, with God, and with creation. Broken relationships are the symptom of what is ultimately a spiritual issue. Sin damages and distorts our relationships.

Restoring relationships takes love. I tend to think of loving God and loving my neighbor as two separate tasks, but as Myers states, they are "twin injunctions of a single command."[13] What does it really mean to combine loving God and loving others?

In my relationship with Wheaton Academy, I have seen a glimpse of loving God and loving others in this more singular and connected model. As the story of Wheaton Academy's response to the AIDS pandemic has unfolded, it has happened in the context of relationships. We decided to visit the community where the new school had been built to meet the students and families who were being impacted by it. Their need went from being a story on a page or brochure, to people with names, children with hopes, dreams, and with much to offer.

This has in turn deeply impacted our own relationships with God. We've seen Him in a new way, getting to know parts of His character in experience, more than just descriptors. We know Him more as our hearts have been broken by the things that break His heart.

What I have found in working with Wheaton Academy is that the original step of faith that I took by meeting with Chip and supporting their efforts would be required of me again and again. Much of what has happened in our relationship has been outside of the organizational box, and has required new approaches, taking risks, and building trust. And in the midst of it all, I find myself feeling like Simon Peter, who after doubting Jesus' direction to put his nets down for a catch, was overwhelmed by the size of the catch, fell on his knees, and said:

"Go away from me, Lord; I am a sinful man!" (Luke 5:8)[14]

Who is this God who calls us into relationship with Himself and others, and who provides for our needs in the process? Seeing Him work through young people has renewed my faith and encouraged me in this work of fundraising for the poor. And it has increased my desire to know Him more. Thank you, Wheaton Academy, for being obedient, and for changing the lives of so many of us along the way.

Tony Frank has been a major gifts fundraiser with World Vision Chicago since 2001. In 2009 he assumed the role of Senior Area Director, and builds relationships on behalf of World Vision with major donors in Illinois, Michigan, and Wisconsin. Tony has led World Vision trips to Mexico, Honduras, Swaziland, and Zambia.

CHAPTER 5

CHANGING AND CREATING A CULTURE

I am often amazed at the myriad of perceptions various groups of people have about an evangelical institution like a Christian school. We can be viewed as being elitist, spoiled, dogmatic, idealistic, or even out of touch by those in the larger culture. We even encounter a vastly different set of expectations concerning what the school should do for their children as we interact with parents both before and during their educational years at a place like Wheaton Academy. Some people believe that we should be an academic powerhouse that prepares students to get into the top-tier colleges that will set them up for future positions of influence and power in our society. Some hope that their kids will excel in athletics and garner the all-important college scholarship as they become well known and admired for what they do on the field or the court. Some want their children to be protected from the temptations and sin that exists in today's teenage world so they can emerge unscathed from their high school years. Some hope that their kids will connect with role model teachers who can speak truth and wisdom into their lives as they see their own voice becoming less influential. Some hope that their kids will move forward in a pursuit of becoming the next leaders of the church that will spread the hope and love of Jesus to their own community and the world beyond suburban Chicago.

In many ways, these vastly different and often changing expectations and perceptions help to shape a culture that often struggles to latch onto one clear and overarching identity. We've believed deeply in trying to be a Christian community and school that welcomes and is a place of connection for students and families with all kinds of interests and needs. We do still end up wrestling with the challenge of functioning as a community and culture so focused on our own achievements and desires that we are unaware and uninvolved in the lives and struggles of people outside our worlds. I have so often been overwhelmed by my tendency to see life through the grid of how each decision and event affects just me and the circle of people closest to me. There is this very powerful notion that if you focus specifically on yourself and doing everything you can to enhance and improve your own life you will be able to create a healthy and happy existence. And in a school setting where the tuition cost runs well into the five-figure range, we are often tempted to believe that we must focus on ourselves and our own programs in order to deliver a product that helps to prepare students for a successful future while keeping them spiritually alive at the same time.

As the administrator and leader responsible for the spiritual life and health of the school and student body, (and who really wants that impossible job, I might add!) I helped to create a culture filled with all kinds of programs that were very good at offering opportunities for our students to grow personally in their relationships with Jesus. We had Bible studies and prayer groups for each of the four classes, all-school chapel services twice weekly, student mentor groups, leadership development teams and trips, overseas mission trips, different Bible classes for each grade, special worship nights, and even Spiritual Life Weeks on the yearly calendar. Many things were offered to help the individual spiritual knowledge and growth of our students with the belief and hope that consistently offered spiritual input would help our students become more like Jesus and that our overall school culture would reflect the character of Christ to the world.

Many of these activities were meaningful and so many of our students had a strong belief in Jesus and a desire to share the Good News Jesus brought to the world as they left our community as Wheaton Academy graduates. Yet our school couldn't seem to shake our reputation as a somewhat aloof and arrogant group of wealthy Christian kids who did fewer bad things, but didn't necessarily care a whole lot about people and needs outside of their own school and "perfect little Christian bubble."

In many ways I was culpable for our focus and even our reputation as the appointed spiritual leader, but together with a group of students we began to reexamine the words of Jesus. In Matthew 22, He first answers a religious leader's question about which was the greatest commandment with a restatement of the Shema in Deuteronomy 6, "You must love the LORD your God with all your heart, all your soul, and all your mind." Almost everything we were doing at Wheaton Academy was focused on this ultimate biblical command. Yet in this interaction, Jesus continued to speak, quoting from Leviticus 19 stating that a second commandment, "Love your neighbor as yourself" was equally important.[15]

In seeking to become people who followed Jesus' words and example, it was quite obvious that we needed to embrace the second piece of Jesus' response to see the real spiritual transformation of our lives and our school culture that we so desired to see. And as God brought to us the needs of a community on the other side of the world, He nudged us and redefined for us what it meant to truly love others and who our neighbor was in the world we lived in. When we began to create ideas that would help us respond to those suffering from poverty and AIDS in Zambia we saw a spiritual response we never expected we would get from our students.

You see, what began as a small group of students trying to convince their friends and classmates of their responsibility to care for their "neighbors" in Africa eventually became that which on a programmatic and heart level overwhelmed and overtook our campus life. The Zambia Project was not just another informational experience where some high school kids learned about a place they had never heard of before. It morphed into something that would not only grab the attention of all types of students in our community, but moved hundreds of them to an active faith response to the very command Jesus Himself said was most important for us to follow. The Spirit of the One who commanded us to love our neighbors fell upon our little suburban school and the culture simply had no choice but to change as God's people fell in love with a group of people in a village far, far away. That love stirred in the teenage world a response that fit who they were and whom God longed for them to become.

It is hard for me to try and explain exactly what this change at Wheaton Academy looked like in some ways. Students still looked pretty much the same and participated in many of the same things as before. But the activities of our school demonstrated a remarkable change as students were given the green light to use their resources, ideas, gifts, and passions to try together to raise money for the restoration of one of the most physically devastated places on the planet. And we had a string of years where a gang of high school kids became one of World Vision Chicago's largest donors as they raised over $100,000 each school year through their new ideas and ventures.

Here is a Top Ten List snapshot of how life on and off our campus shifted from a self-focus in DuPage County to a focus on others who lived in north central Zambia:

Creation and execution of over one hundred different student-run fundraisers:

We turned our student body loose to try to create all kinds of simple events that other students would want to be a part of in order to raise funds for our specific projects each year. Typically, a student had an interest in a particular activity and then set up an event that other Wheaton Academy students and their friends could come to and pay a fee that would go toward helping to build a new school, medical clinic and equipment, child evangelism ministry center, or clean water wells in the Kakolo Village community. The events were student created, developed, promoted, and run. My job was typically to answer questions via text along the way, show up as a participant, and put the money collected into our Zambia account afterward. We discovered that our students loved the notion that their social life could be scripted in such a way that it would change the lives of people in need in Africa, even while they were doing something they enjoyed with their friends back in America. Some of our most creative and most successful grassroots fundraisers have included:

Biggest Loser: Twelve male faculty members entered a weight loss contest for one hundred days and students pledged per pound for the faculty member they believed would lose the most weight. The group lost over 400 pounds, including 150 pounds between the headmaster and principal of the school, and over $15,000 was collected for the construction of a maternity ward where women could give birth safely instead of having a baby under a tree in their village.

Bench for Zambia: Wearing shirts with the motto "lifting the weight of poverty" motivating them, several regulars in our weight room bench-pressed thousands of pounds and raised over $4,000 in pledges to help purchase HIV testing equipment for a new medical clinic.

President's Day 3 V 3 Soccer Tourney: Many teams of both soccer and non-soccer players from Wheaton Academy competed in a day-long tournament that also included teams from other area high schools and colleges battling through a round-robin indoor competition. For some strange reason the Wheaton Academy faculty/coaches team has been the perennial champ in this event. Close to $5,000 has been raised to help build a school where the African children now play soccer (futball) in PE classes every Friday and enjoy the game that they and their whole country adore and never tire of playing on dirt fields with wooden goalposts.

Climbing Mount Rainier: A couple of faculty members and a small group of current and former students who had been involved in our school's Adventure Club program peaked one of the most challenging mountains in the US just outside Seattle and raised over $20,000 through sponsors to provide clean water for the school, medical clinic, and hundreds of families in Kakolo Village. One of the Wheaton Academy students collected snow from the peak in a Nalgene that he mixed with the first drops of clean water from the new well in Zambia the following summer. His picture holding a Zambia flag on the top of the mountain ended up in a World Vision publication seen by hundreds of thousands of their faithful supporters.

Wheaton Academy Football Shirts: We raised close to $5,000 to help install electricity for the village school and medical clinic by designing and then distributing Wheaton Academy football shirts to over five hundred students and alumni from the school. The only catch was that we didn't have a football program at the time! We did put on the back "Undefeated since 1989" because that is when the last game was played by a team with thirteen players who lost their final game of the year 84-0.

Mongolian BBQ Guest Grillers Night: A handful of students and teachers got to cook the food ordered by customers at a popular downtown restaurant in the trendy suburb of Naperville one night to help raise money to provide long-term food security for areas in Zambia affected by a deadly famine season. While we stood over a two thousand-degree grill with tongs flipping stir-fry and burning our knuckles our students collected over $1,000 in tip jars as they told customers waiting for their food about our passion to help the poor receive food in Zambia.

African Bracelet Sale: On several trips to Zambia our students and other friends bought African copper bracelets made with Zambia's key natural resource. After purchasing them from local traders in the market, we would then sell them to students and parents to wear as a reminder to daily pray for the people of Zambia who had made what they were wearing on their wrists. A couple thousand dollars was collected to help fund microfinance loans for entrepreneurs of shops back in Zambia.

So many others: Other fun, creative, and meaningful endeavors included a fast called the 30 Hour Famine to help with the hunger crisis; a spring car wash run by the senior class at a local funeral home parking lot; Mario Kart for Zambia with video game races projected onto our big screen at school; a dodgeball tournament where a big circle with the word poverty was the target on the shirts worn by participants; penny wars between classes as part of the homecoming competition; and neighborhood workdays where students volunteered their services to do all kinds of jobs for families in the subdivisions near the school in exchange for a donation to the Zambia Project.

Wheaton Academy Zambia Auction:

Many private schools like ours host auction events, inviting some of their wealthy parents, alums, and friends to come to an event featuring great food and many luxury items that can be bid on to benefit the school's annual fund or improvements on the current campus. Our students helped along with a parent team to put on an auction that told the story in pictures of the needs in sub-Saharan Africa and also shared stories of how our student community had responded to God's call to be His answer to their prayers. One of our friends from Zambia was making the native staple food of enshema in the kitchen as the caterer ran around her, and one of the items that stimulated a bidding war was a beautiful portrait of an African orphan done by an artist who had recently visited Zambia. Over $50,000 was split between funds for a medical clinic to help prevent the passing on of the HIV virus from moms to their newborn children and scholarships for Wheaton Academy students who continue to dream of how they can change the world during their high school years.

Curriculum development and integration:

Our response to the AIDS pandemic had caused us to see that the issues of poverty, economics, social justice, colonization, and globalization must be talked about in a Christian school classroom. Our business classes were now talking about the Millennium Development Goals and the impact of microfinance loans; our history and government classes discussed African history and the connections between Africa and our everyday lives; our Bible classes looked at the themes of justice and equality in the Scriptures while highlighting the influence of the global church; and I've even taught an intensive class focusing on the major poverty and social justice topics in the world today. This class was developed because students were hungry to become more equipped to be a credible voice in the culture as they live as leaders who advocate for the lives at great risk across the globe.

Personal student sacrifices and gifts:

The heart of the cultural shift at our school has not only come in new and creative events, as cool and creative as they have become; the real transformation has been displayed in the individual student decisions to live differently than they did before. One Monday morning one of our teacher champions of the project asked the faculty to contribute out of their own pockets to a pot of money he was gathering to then distribute unequally to our students during an upcoming chapel service on stewardship. When each student walked into chapel they found an envelope with anywhere between $1 and $20 taped on the bottom of their seats. After this teacher's powerful testimony about his personal journey toward giving more freely of what God had given him, he invited the students to come to the stage if they wanted and give the free money they had received back so it could help with the construction of a new medical clinic. They could also keep it and no one would know, or even add to it out of what they currently had in their own possession. We watched hundreds of students silently file up to the stage and when we counted the money it was almost double what had been taped under the seats! We teachers who gave saw what God will do through a student example of taking a gift and multiplying it as an even greater gift to those who truly need it.

An early phrase one of our senior guys coined in the history of the project was "your change makes change" and we began to create opportunities for students to deposit their spare change at various places around school. We put a little can with a cut hole on the top next to our vending machines, put plastic jugs at the end of our cafeteria lunch line, and handed out little paper houses in which students could collect change for a month or so and then return. (We loved it when they were so full that they came back reinforced with strips of duct tape!) One of my funniest memories of my last few years is marching into my bank with several of my biggest senior guys lugging in duffel bags of change to be counted at the bank. The teller's expression was something between utter shock and horror, and she quietly said, "Can I get your phone number? I'll call you in a couple of days with the total if the counting machine doesn't break." We've collected enough change (maybe $20,000 or so) over the years to help change the educational future of hundreds of future Zambian community contributors and leaders.

Perhaps the most powerful example of student sacrifice I've observed has been in relationship to a sacred part of the high school experience. It is an American rite of passage of sorts to go out and buy a spectacular dress if you are a girl attending your junior/senior prom during your high school years. At our school, girls start the thinking and searching process for that elusive dress months before the actual event is held during the second weekend in May. A few of our girls began to think about the hundreds of dollars regularly spent on dresses that were typically worn only for a handful of hours before being put in a closet and never worn again. They did something somewhat unthinkable in their worlds. They decided they didn't need to buy a new dress to go to their prom. In fact, they decided that the amount of money they would spend on a dress could go toward helping girls their age in Zambia have healthy deliveries of their babies in a clinic so far away from the prom scene back at home. They created something called the Zambia dress exchange so girls could still get a new dress without paying for it at a store. They asked girls at Wheaton Academy to bring in their formal dresses sitting in their closets and then created a "dress store" of sorts where girls and even their moms could come in on a Saturday and pick out a dress one of their classmates had donated for another to wear. Many young ladies looked beautiful in their pictures on a sunny Saturday afternoon celebrating one of the big events of high school wearing designer dresses they hadn't paid for. Beautiful young ladies in Kakolo Village sat thanking God for the sacrifices that helped them to hold a healthy, HIV negative baby in their arms on the same night while girls ate and danced and laughed on the other side of the world.

Yearly spring traditions of Mr. Wheaton Academy and 5K Run:

Each spring we put on two major events that draw big crowds and are great memory makers for those who participate and attend. Mr. Wheaton Academy is a student event that features fifteen senior guys competing for a coveted title. Each of them dresses in a specially themed outfit, performs a unique talent, and is featured in several group dance numbers. Contestants and the senior girls who help choreograph the dance moves put in a few months of work preparing for this one night that sells out our Fine Arts Center and raises thousands of dollars and generates lots of screams and laughs along the way. Near the end of May we also host a 5K Run titled the Run for Hungry Children where we partner with Bright Hope International to feed starving children in Zambia. We have created a course that runs in and out and all over our school campus. Our cross country runners battle it out with area local runners for first place in the run. Many of our students and families run with hundreds of others from the church that meets on weekends on our campus to make a different life for those who often walk much more than five kilometers to and from school each day.

Hands-on gathering of supplies and building of caregiver kits and school supply bags:

One of the challenges we faced every day was helping our students in Chicago believe, and to a certain extent, feel that they were personally involved in this work God seemed to be doing on our campus. When some of our students traveled to Zambia, they were obviously struck with the tangible reality of poverty and the new understanding of how small items in our stores and home cabinets could meet some of the greatest needs of the people of Kakolo. This caused them to come up with new ideas that would involve gathering those specific items rather than just raising resources for the big ticket community projects we often promoted.

World Vision had established a program where Zambians from local churches and community groups began to care personally for the needs of those suffering from HIV/AIDS in rural contexts. These "caregivers" often spent hours each week visiting and providing simple medical care and vital relational love and prayers for those who were suffering and dying without anyone else around to care for them. The World Vision team created a "caregiver kit" concept where churches and other organizations were invited to purchase the supplies and then build these kits that would be given to African caregivers to provide them with the supplies needed to better care for those they were visiting as representatives of the Savior who loves those who suffer alone.

Our students decided that we would create a contest during homecoming week where they would challenge each of the four high school classes to go out and purchase different items that would be put into each caregiver kit. Items included things like soap, Vaseline, flashlights, aspirin, washcloths, and a notebook. Several pharmacies in the area ran out of anti-fungal cream and I ended up having to order a case of it from walgreens.com. Each class brought in over five hundred of each of the eight items making up a kit and stacked them in our multi-purpose room on campus. We then took a normal chapel time and had each student personally put together a caregiver kit and write a note telling the caregiver they would be praying for them as they cared for the least in our world, often at great cost to themselves. I still remember vividly shrink-wrapping hundreds and hundreds of caregiver kits as we put them on a World Vision truck that would ultimately place them in the hands of our heroes on the other side of the world.

A couple of years later a few of our students were giving some school supply items like paper and pencils we had collected from some school families and churches to the headmaster of the Kakolo Village school. He began to tear up as they dropped the items on his desk, and then shared with the students that their budget for school supplies for the year was $50, just enough to typically purchase chalk for the blackboards for one semester. On the plane ride home, some notes were scribbled into a spiral notebook and another homecoming project was birthed. This time each class purchased different school supply items that each Wheaton Academy student then individually put into an orange drawstring bag with Kakolo School printed on the outside. Each bag was filled with about a dozen simple school supply items never seen before by Zambian students and a note from a high school kid across the ocean encouraging them to keep pursuing the education that would dramatically change their life.

The following summer a couple of huge boxes arrived at a schoolhouse in Zambia. On a windy June day, about twenty Wheaton Academy students and teachers spent a couple of hours personally presenting six hundred students a school supply bag. I can't forget the screams and songs and claps that rose up from the lines of students when the Zambian community leaders announced that each student would receive this gift. I loved seeing little girls walk back to their little family hut with the big and bright orange bag hanging down on their backs. And I loved it even more when a few years later those bags were still strung on student shoulders as they walked to their classrooms each morning as the sun came up in their African village.

Least: a fine arts festival highlighting the needs and celebrating the lives of the least of these in our world today:

For the past several years, we have put on a fine arts festival where hundreds of student artists use the arts to express their thoughts and feelings regarding God's love for and concern for the least in our world today. Students and guest artists have used the mediums of music, visual art, photography, graphic arts, video, poetry, and dramatic sketches to demonstrate both the need and the response to those suffering from disease, oppression, injustice, and lack of resources in our world. And there has been a beautiful strain of response highlighting the beauty and value and giftedness of the least many of us have gotten to know as people rather than just victims of bad choices or difficult conditions. Here are the titles of a few of our years of focused response from our student artists:

Artists Respond to Poverty and AIDS

Made in the Image of God: A Response to the Need for Justice and Equality

A Change in Me: Artists Impacted by Relationships with the Least

World Vision AIDS Experience Exhibit:

One of the unique challenges for students passionate about this remarkable Kingdom work going on at their particular school was trying to appropriately and most effectively share that passion to invite others to be a part of the response to the needs so clearly present in communities being impacted by the HIV/AIDS pandemic. Our friends at World Vision actually came up with a remarkable tool to aid in the task of helping those connected to the Wheaton Academy student body understand why we cared so much about a place far away and a disease seemingly not present in our daily lives.

They developed a portable African village that was brought in a huge semi truck and then set up in one of our main meeting areas on our campus. I remember telling World Vision this particular stop on the AIDS Experience Tour would be a little unique because it would be staffed by teenagers rather than church member adults. I know they were a little nervous at first, but over two hundred high school students spent a week talking about and helping close to three thousand other folks walk through the experience of what it was like to be a child in an African village whose life was forever affected by the HIV virus. I watched with joy as parents of hundreds of students understood for the first time why their son or daughter wanted to talk about and give to people facing tremendous suffering on another continent. And I loved the chance to have a host of students from other public and private schools and area churches be moved to action after getting a small taste of what it is like to walk in another person's shoes. We closed the week with a banquet where our students simply and eloquently shared their passions, their experiences, and their dreams for a new schoolhouse addition with parents and other World Vision friends and donors from around Chicago so that even more students could break the AIDS cycle and stigma through the power of education.

So many T-shirts!:

With so many Zambia events and fundraisers we have created a flurry of colorful T-shirts representing the vast array of events that have gone on in our campus life. During the 2004-05 school year one of our teachers counted them up and determined that over thirty Zambia Project T-shirts had been made and then worn around campus by our students. One of my former students recently gave me a large fleece blanket made up of close to twenty of those T-shirts that I wrap around me and remember my friends needing a blanket like this on the other side of the world.

Bricks with names of Kakolo students lining the walkway outside the Wheaton Academy school entrance:

As the last group of senior students, connected for their whole Wheaton Academy educational experience to the Zambia Project graduated, they came up with one final project that would in their minds forever link our students to the students at the Kakolo Village school in Zambia. They asked me to send an e-mail to one of the school officials in Zambia requesting a list of the names of all the students who attended the K-9 school in our little community. After a few weeks, I got an e-mail with all of the names of the students in the school. They have lists of them posted in the schoolhouse itself in Zambia. The idea they had was to invite our students to purchase a brick and then paint their name and the name of a Zambian student they selected from the list together on the brick itself. If you walk around the front atrium of Wheaton Academy today, you will see a sidewalk made from bricks. These bricks were put in the ground by students from privilege in Chicago who wrote an African name next to their own because they truly believed that God had changed both of their lives through His connecting work between them. That connection ran so deep that they believed it had to be and will be felt by generations of students who attend Wheaton Academy and read the names on those bricks in the years to come.

In Luke 14, Jesus talks with some really privileged and important cultural and religious leaders about who they should invite to their parties as he eats dinner with them at one of their homes. He tells them they shouldn't invite people who can bring good food and drink to the party or who will help raise the status of the party in the local social scene. In fact, they shouldn't even invite people who will be easy to talk to and please because they are just like them. He exhorts them to invite the poor, the sick, the dirty, the disenfranchised to their gatherings—and He promises them that they will be blessed if they invite these types of folks to the parties they throw.

I think we obviously look toward the blessing and reward Jesus will offer us at the end of our lives for our faithful service to those He cares deeply about. But I have learned that this blessing isn't just someday—it is very much for today and tomorrow as well. It still seems somewhat counterintuitive to seek to build a student culture at any school or youth group or team setting around serving the least in our world today. In a generation connected technologically almost every minute of the day with unprecedented choices and products and experiences, it really is hard to fathom that shifting a culture radically would produce such real and robust fruit in the lives of individual students and student communities. Yet my own testimony is that the things you have read about in this chapter were ridiculously fun, remarkably captivating, and incredibly life-giving. This has blessed students in ways they never dreamed, and made our student culture what we secretly believed it could and should be. The words of the One who said we would find ourselves blessed in our service and filled to overflowing as a result of caring for the poor and the needy have indeed rung true in a generation of twenty-first century young Christians. And I am still convinced today that serving and loving one another near and far is indeed the best way to change the way the evangelical community is perceived. The truth of Jesus' words in John 13:35 have been demonstrated to indeed be fully true as He told His followers as He prepared to leave them,

> *"All people will know that you are my disciples, if you have love for one another."[16]*

ENTERING IN WITH THE LEAST

Ryan Souders

Although I'm not certain you have heard of the area, I am from a small suburb just west of a major city in the Midwest of the United States. Churches are everywhere, Bible studies are visible in the local coffee shops, and it even boasts of a prestigious Christian university, which I attended. Nowhere else in the country, maybe the world, is Christianity "practiced" and viewed with such high regard, respect, and in reality, ease. There is more or less a certain way to do things, a certain way to act, and most certainly a way to "Do Christian."

If you had to peg it, Christianity here looks something like this: a two-parent household with a father who works in some form of finance job and stunning wife who works out in some sort of health club. Their two kids most definitely attend the Christian elementary school and are the smartest, most athletic, best musicians you have ever met. The family owns two cars (that is until the kids are old enough to drive) and financial worry is far from their minds. They all attend a local church on Sunday mornings. By in large, these are good people, with good motives, whom I truly believe honestly and earnestly love Jesus and want to follow Him.

And in that, there is no wrong. It is apparent that God is active and moving in this, and other communities like it. Families give their first fruits and hold true to Joshua's mantra that *"As for me and my house, we will serve the LORD."*[17] God has given and blessed abundantly, allowing vats and barns to overflow again and again. It is this very place that I myself grew up and am in absolutely no hurry to leave.

And yet still there was something missing.

Have you seen the movie *Hook*? It's a favorite of mine. Robin Williams plays Peter Pan, Julia Roberts is Tinker Bell. In this modern version of the age-old fairy tale, Pan's kids get taken from the real world and he has to go back to Never Never Land in order to rescue them. Upon his return Peter lives with his former companions as they at first refuse to believe it is, in fact, he who has come back to them. The boys have moved on. They have a new leader. They have new battles with Hook. All in all, things are good.

In one scene Peter sits down with the boys for dinner. There is no food before them and yet the boys scarf down nothing like it's a Thanksgiving feast. Confused, Peter asks what is going on and the boys confess they haven't been eating like they used to. To save you some sappy dialogue, the boys encourage Peter to "imagine." Low and behold, he does and a smorgasbord of real food comes into focus and the boys start feasting with enough left over to have a massive food fight.

You see, I am a product of this "Do Christian" environment. As a matter of fact, it allowed me to attend a private Christian high school, one that called itself an Academy. By the time I was a second semester freshman, I could "do it" just as well as anyone else. I learned the songs, knew the answers, and was a decent enough athlete to turn some heads. For three years in some weird way, I was a king of sorts at this Christian high school. We all were. I was even selected to be on Project LEAD, an elite group of senior leaders who sat around, drank coffee, and read and thought Christian.

I had no idea it would ruin my life.

If you have made it this far, you already know the details of how this project started. You know it has been a bunch of high school students and graduates who have had a ridiculous impact on behalf of the Kingdom of God and have watched it forcefully explode both in their own community and on the other side of the world.

You know that part of the story is the money—over half a million dollars raised by students.

You know that this, as much as anything else, put this Academy on the map.

You also know the impact it has had on one of the Academy's primary leaders and thinkers.

What you don't know, however, is how the Kingdom of God showed up and had greater impact on those individuals than they could ever offer the Kingdom in return. You see, whenever the term Kingdom of God or Kingdom of Heaven appears in the Scriptures, it is always compared to something; it is always like something. The Kingdom of God is like a mustard seed. It is like a man who found a pearl. It is like so many things, and yet we are never exactly told what it is. There are no real specifics. We just know that when we find it, we should do any and everything we can to chase after it and take hold of it.

The Jewish idea of heaven is just that, an idea. It wasn't necessarily some place that we were to be taken away to after we die if we said a prayer. Instead, heaven is the idea that things were the way God wanted them to be, the way they were always supposed to be. Consider Jesus' signs and wonders. When he shows up on the scene and things are as Jesus wants them to be, amazing things happen. Blind people see. Lame people walk. Water is turned into wine. In a very real way, we read about heaven on earth.

I have seen this in the eyes of widows and the smiles of orphans during my two trips to Africa. And in my time among these people we have "helped" I have seen remarkable community that can exist among the body of believers. I have seen the reality that laughter has no language barrier, and ultimately hope blossoms when things are placed under the rule and reign of Christ.

What I have been able to see, realize, and live is that today we have the opportunity to bring heaven to earth. Christ himself opened up this opportunity for us. When we choose to enter in, to live, and to help things exist as God wants them to we are helping to usher in the Kingdom just as He did thousands of years ago.

I have come to see that Jesus' instructions in the Gospels are not just some ideal set of practices to sit around and debate. Jesus' instructions to

His followers as Dallas Willard writes were "instructions in a new way of living. To not listen and obey them would be foolish."[18] You see, people in Jesus' day saw His instructions as life-giving. From day one God has heard the cry of His oppressed people. One could certainly live without understanding this principle, but to grasp it would be like finding a pearl in a large field, and living it out could be what allows the lame to walk and the blind to see.

Being a part of this Kingdom wouldn't take away from, but rather add to the fullness of daily life, and it would help us understand more of who we have been created to be. To enter in to relationship, to experience community, changes us from the inside out. For some it has been working in local community shelters. For me, it has been the relationship with a community that has allowed me to interact and support my sponsored brother, Lloyd—to see him grow up in spite of an AIDS ravaged home that has taken both his parents and to see that there is for him, too, a promise of a hope and a future.

It is in the midst of this reality that I find I have been living like Peter Pan's Lost Boys. For years I sat around and was completely satisfied with fake food. I ate it up, all of it. I got up and went about things like everyone else. I had quiet time devotions, attended small groups, went to church, and did everything I was supposed to do. And these have had significant value, irreplaceable value in my life.

Yet once I got ahold of that real food, I have never been the same. It fills me up like nothing I have ever had before. Its taste is like nothing I have ever tried. And most incredibly, there is always more than enough.

In a sense God showed up and whispered the exact same line in my own ear, "Imagine!" Imagine what it would be like if we actually ate, all of us. Imagine what heaven on earth would look like. Imagine what things could be if they were as I AM wanted them to be.

Ryan is a graduate of Wheaton College and has been involved in professional and collegiate soccer as a player, coach, and front office staff member.

CHAPTER 6

RELATIONSHIPS ACROSS THE OCEAN

I have spent the last few years writing about what God invited us to do as a student community over eight years in response to the AIDS pandemic in Zambia. As I retell the story in my typing of words, the memories invariably draw me to sneak a peek in my saved computer photos at many of the African faces I have gotten to know and love over that time frame. You see, my own life and faith now is deeply intertwined with these faces and their stories. I've spent a good portion of my life trying to teach in such a way that it changes and transforms the lives of the students sitting in my office, classroom, soccer pitch, youth group room, mountain top vista, or retreat cabin. I've desperately wanted them to hear and embrace the things that truly matter, the key biblical principles they really need to learn, and for them to experience all the fullness of life Jesus overcame death in order to bring into their lives today.

In the midst of all that teaching, I have found myself still being taught about what is most important in this life as well. Several years ago there was an extremely popular book written by Robert Fulghum entitled *All I Really Need to Know I Learned in Kindergarten*, and his list of findings included these kinds of phrases:

Play fair.
Don't hit people.
Put things back where you found them.
Clean up your own mess.
Don't take things that aren't yours.
Say you're sorry when you hurt somebody.
Wash your hands before you eat.
Flush.
Warm cookies and cold milk are good for you.
Take a nap every afternoon.[19]

This book sold millions of copies and I remember getting one from a relative when I graduated from college. But if I were to write my own little book about this very topic twenty years after receiving these pearls of wisdom, my title would be *All I Ever Really Needed to Know I Learned in Zambia.* Here's a dozen statements I've come to believe after having them taught to me from the other side of the world:

Living without a watch or clock is a rather freeing way to live.

I don't know if you've ever been in a place where there are no clocks on any walls or watches on people's wrists or cell phones in people's pockets. It is disturbing at first. However, after the initial panic you actually begin to cherish the notion that you can talk without one of you glancing at the time you have left to converse. You can build your schedule around the needs of life that come up as you live each day rather than missing out on opportunities for ministry, friendship, and unique experiences because the time says you have to move on to the next meeting or task. You can tell the whole story of an event in your life and be free to then listen to the story of response without having to just get the facts or details. Time becomes an asset rather than an interrupter in doing things that seem to really matter.

Share freely even if you don't have extra on hand when you give things away.

The daily income of many of the families of Kakolo Village is equal to the three quarters and a dime we don't even notice in our pockets or car console. Yet in the midst of having so little, their giving is extravagant.

When we first came to the village in 2004, different people in the village gave us live chickens and ducks as expressions of gratitude for the help we had provided in building the new school building. As I gingerly held a chicken waiting for it to attack me, I quickly figured out that this bird represented perhaps the most valuable possession a local family had now given to me. It could produce eggs to sell at the market or could be eaten as a valued delicacy. Very few people in this community had even one chicken. And it was given with reverence and blessing when the woman handing it to me literally fell to the ground as she gave it to me. I've never received a gift that represented more economic or personal value than the chicken. The giver of that gift had less than anyone who had ever given me a present.

Dance when the Spirit of God moves inside of you.

The high school and colleges where I have worked recently have chosen to allow dances as social activities. Many Christian schools don't have a prom in the spring; they have a junior/senior banquet with food and skits and videos, but no band or DJ. I don't go to a church that has people dancing except for a few folks who are clapping and exhibiting a slight bit of sway in the hips or tapping of the feet during our worship song time. But every time I am in Africa, there is absolutely no doubt that I will be dancing. I will be dancing at church, dancing before a big dinner, and dancing whenever we dedicate a new building or program that will serve to save and improve the quality of lives in this community.

I don't consider myself someone with the natural gift of rhythm. I really struggle in church to clap and sing and stay on beat when doing both. But when the people of Africa start to dance in response to something God has done or provided, I am often the first one in our group to jump up and join them. I would be ashamed and embarrassed to have my friends see me dance in America, but I am strangely freed to move my feet and body in Zambia as a response of worship and joy and freedom. All the Old Testament passages talking about the Israelites and even their leaders like King David dancing before and in response to God suddenly made sense to me like never before.

One such moment occurred during a community church service in Kakolo. Two of our girls, who are good dancers, danced in the dirt of Zambia to Bono and Alicia Keys singing "Don't Give Up (Africa)" while the hundreds and hundreds of Zambians whooped and hollered and ran to joyfully fan them with their clothes. The Spirit of the Lord hovered among us in a way where we could literally sense the very presence of God as His people danced in affirmation that He was still there, still at work, and still loved all of us on that Sunday morning in an African village.

Learn all you can because it is a privilege to receive an education.

There isn't a day and barely an hour that goes by at our high school where students don't groan or sigh or roll their eyes at the notion that they have to spend five days a week being forced to try and learn and become educated. Education feels like an obligation rather than an opportunity for many of them who have grown bored after years of being in school. Many college students paying hundreds of thousands of dollars for an education regularly read and write posts on Facebook rather than listen to what is being taught in their classrooms.

In Zambia, we wondered what would happen when we funded the construction of a two-room schoolhouse in a community where most of the children had never had the chance to go to school before. Within a few years eight hundred children were registered and ready to come to school in the two rooms now available. To accommodate all who wanted to come and learn, the students were slotted into morning or afternoon shifts and could attend on certain days of the week based on their grade level. Many of the children in Zambia walked several miles each way to get an education, sometimes leaving before sunrise or getting home after dark. When observing their classrooms there is a palpable sense that they must listen intently because what they hear may very well change the direction and course of their lives. When we saw the level of passion and interest in becoming educated, we knew we had to help fund a major schoolhouse addition so that the children of Kakolo can learn.

And what a privilege we have to learn in truly remarkable settings at Wheaton Academy or Cornerstone University while being part of bringing lasting change to villages in Zambia through the opportunity to learn in a simple schoolhouse on an African plain.

When friends come to visit, run out to greet them.

I am amazed that oftentimes when my neighbor or someone I know rings my doorbell to come and say hello, to ask for a favor, or to share something going on in his or her life (which really doesn't happen very often because my garage and doors are usually firmly shut) I make my children check and see who it is and contemplate having them make an excuse for why I am not available to be interrupted. The funny part is that when I do open the door, I am often blessed by what he or she says or brings or even needs in the context of our relationship.

I have viewed the power and value of hospitality somewhat differently since being welcomed in a rather unique way in Zambia. Each time that our little minibus vehicle chugs down that long dirt road and begins to drive right through the huts and brick homes on each side of the road, children and many of their parents begin to scream and yell and wave at their friends from Chicago who have now come to see them again. There are hundreds of children who begin to sprint to either run alongside the vehicle or take a shortcut to the spot where they know we will stop. We are almost always greeted with a song of welcome and blessing, and we often can barely open the bus door because of the number of folks crowded around the stopped vehicle.

During our visits to the community over a week's time, this welcome is repeated with the same energy level every single day. The village leaders are always there with a hug, a gift, and a formal welcome presentation. For some of us, old friends break through the mass to tell us how good it is to be together once again. It's rather strange sometimes when you begin to think thoughts that this actually feels a little, or maybe even a lot, like we are coming home. And that African gift of biblical hospitality has caused me to travel tens of thousands of miles to see my friends again and again and again.

When your family member is sick or in crisis, drop everything and do anything to care for that person and his or her needs.

Many Americans who I know do just about everything they can do to avoid going to the doctor or the hospital to get treated when something is wrong with their physical body; most Africans only dream of being able to go to the pediatrician or hospital with the latest technically advanced medical equipment that helps bring healing to the sick. Illness is seen as a bother in the States while disease in Zambia threatens to overwhelm families, communities, and even the nation in many ways. There is a saying everyone believes to be true in

Zambia in regards specifically to the HIV virus that says "either you are infected or affected by AIDS in this country." I've been in huts where mothers are taking care of their dying children, and I've been in brick homes where the children are taking care of their dying parents. I've never heard complaints, just requests for prayers, for medicines, and for help in these seemingly hopeless situations.

The majority of my healthy friends in Zambia have other relatives, most often children, living with them in cramped spaces due to the loss of life of one of their siblings or parents. Jesus-like compassion may never be shown more clearly than when a young girl or boy drops out of school to be the caretaker of their dying mom or dad who should be caring for them. One of my good friends from Zambia told of how she as a young teenage girl had to carry her dying father on her back to the medical clinic several miles away so he could possibly receive some medicines that particular day. I've watched what family truly means in an African village. I can only hope and pray my level of unselfishness and sacrificial care will creep closer to the same that I've observed up close in Zambia when and if my family members need me to be the one to care for them despite the costs to my own life.

Jesus loves the little children, all the children of the world.

When you ask almost anyone who has gone to Zambia with us about their trip, they will talk first about the kids; the kids who grab your hand when you are walking across the dirt landscape; the kids who have the same clothes on each day you are there and sometimes the same as they had on last year when you last saw them; the kids who sing about Jesus with strong and clear voices; the kids who run for almost a mile chasing your vehicle down the dirt road out of the village; the kids who have eaten once in the last thirty-six hours and still come to school; the kids who often have their younger siblings fastened to their backs as they walk around.

I have a couple of sponsored kids named Peter and Anthony whom I have met and brought small gifts to in Zambia. It is an incredible privilege and joy to meet in person these kids whose pictures are on a refrigerator or bulletin board. As I kick a soccer ball around with them I am laughing outwardly and overwhelmed inwardly as I think about my own children who are the exact same ages as these two energetic little guys. We pass the ball back and forth outside their small one-room homes and I become overwhelmingly convinced that the Savior who welcomed children onto His lap has called me to love children no matter where they have grown up, no matter what their future prospects may hold, no matter if they are infected with a virus, simply because He loves them.

Children in Zambia are at incredible risk and yet represent immense possibility at the same time. The contrast is both startling and compelling as you imagine my kids Olivia and Trey living in Africa, and Peter and Anthony growing up in the American suburbs. If we are to change the course of this nation, if we are to truly make progress on these wildly ambitious Millennium Development Goals set by the United Nations, if we are going to truly welcome all the children into life and hope as Jesus did in the first century while crowds watched Him do so, we must do everything we can to demonstrate with our hands, our money, and our voice that each child is worthy of receiving what they need to become all that God dreams they can become. Someday I plan to take Olivia and Trey to meet Peter and Anthony and Monica and Gracias, the kids we have decided we will try to welcome and serve and resource in the name of Jesus on the other side of the world. My dream is that they will all be healthy, all excited about what they are learning in school, all full of dreams for the future, and all convinced that Jesus loves them each more than they can ever imagine. And I dream for them to be able to do all that God has created them to accomplish in their lifetimes because of the care they received as children.

Water and food and blankets are blessings from heaven.

For the last several years, I've found myself attracted to three specific things here in my world: I love drinking flavored water as opposed to straight "plain" water; I love eating lunch at places like Chipotle, Qdoba, or Baja Fresh; and I love going to bed at night with a fleece blanket on top of me no matter what the temperature is outside. These are my own little quirks and they are probably also enjoyed by thousands, if not millions, of other Americans. Yet I have rarely, if ever, thanked God for the berry taste in my water bottle or mentioned the blessing of well-cooked and flavored chicken while praying for my meal with friends at these restaurants or for the miracle of softness and warmth this magical material called fleece provides for me every night as I lay down and wrap myself deeply into it.

However, after being with my friends in Zambia, even though my attraction to these things remains strong, I am more able to see them as gifts rather than norms in my everyday existence because of the following images that are imbedded in my mind.

I've watched young girls pull water that is not even close to clear, let alone magically endowed with a flavor enhancer, out of a deep hole in the ground using a plastic scoop tied to a rope. This water is full of waterborne organisms she and her family will be exposed to as they bathe and cook and drink with the water from this jug because it is the only source of liquid in a season where it doesn't rain for many months. I've prayed with many, many Zambian friends for rain, the water from heaven that determines whether they will eat or not this coming year. I think I've only prayed for rain a few times so that my brown lawn will look nicer and so that I don't have to do the arduous task of moving the sprinklers around the yard because I don't have an in-ground system like most of my neighbors.

We have tried to make all of our students eat some enshema, the local staple food, while we are traveling in Zambia. It is corn crushed up and then cooked into a paste-like substance heated over a fire in almost every home in the country. It doesn't taste bad yet doesn't taste great. But when I see it cooking in the early afternoon outside a hut where the grandmother is preparing the one meal for the day for herself and the orphans she is caring for, I quickly understand that this provision means more to them than my free-range chicken with the right spice does for me. I now pray daily that God would feed my friends in Zambia, even sometimes with two meals a day, and with an occasional vegetable or piece of meat as a bonus and expression of His love and care to them.

A few summers ago I went to visit a pair of sponsored twins at their small home because some of my best friends, who had just given birth to twins in the US got World Vision to find a set of twins in our community for them to sponsor as they welcomed two lives into their world in Illinois. The Zambian mom was so excited to see the pictures of the twins just born in America and she took me inside to sit and talk in their home. There was one bedroom where the seven people in their family all slept on a cement floor where a thin blanket lay over the ground. I was initially a bit shocked at the idea of seven folks sleeping together, but soon became obsessed with trying to find where another blanket was in the home. As I walked through the whole house trailing behind her, I never saw another one. And I remembered an early morning walk to breakfast one day in June in Zambia where it was just a few degrees above freezing and I wished I had my gray, fleece LeaderTreks blanket to give to this family who depended on God to keep them warm at night.

A short life can still be a full life.

I turned forty a couple of summers ago and received all kinds of cards and wishes talking about the next forty years being even better than the first forty. While I am not yet convinced wholeheartedly that will be the case, especially given my decreasing soccer skills and recent dental work bills, I have been programmed to believe that the next decades of my life may well and probably should be when I contribute most significantly to my family, my workplace, and the world. It is almost like the first "half" of my life was spent mostly in preparation for the moments where I could finally really do something because I had paid my dues and was qualified to do so.

As I read cards and notes on my fortieth birthday I remembered the first time I read the statistic that the average life expectancy in Zambia had dropped to thirty-five years of age. I was deeply troubled during my first visit when I discovered very few people my age.

My time in Zambia has often reminded me that every day is valuable, and that we do not have to live to be old in physical years to have deep spiritual impact and a life full of joy and meaning and purpose. God is using so many young people in Africa to bring about real change to a place that many might have given up on. They are fully experiencing and appreciating life the way we were designed to, regardless of how much time and how many moments or years God gives them on this earth.

A gracious spirit attracts other people to you.

I've found it fascinating that the majority of the people I've travelled with have fallen in love with this little country called Zambia, and e-mail, text, or Facebook me often about how they can't stop thinking about going back there again someday. The most interesting part of that wish is that they never mention any of the tourist places we've visited as spots worthy of being a repeat destination. They only want to return to the Kakolo Village community where they met and got to know people in a relational way. I would argue they are drawn to Africa by the spirit present in the people of Zambia. They may not dress the same as we do or have in their possession material things that we would identify as valuable, but the people of Zambia display an unusually noticeable evidence of the grace of God in their words and in how they interact with us as we come into their community and their lives. There is a gentleness, kindness, and even a joyful laughter in their spirit that is noticeably different than some of the places and relationships we encounter daily in the West. It is this spirit that is so attractive and compelling that it will push a student to leave behind technology, fast food, and daily comforts for the chance to be in the midst of those who embody grace, the grace of a loving God displayed in the midst of poverty perhaps more distinctly than He is in the midst of financial blessing.

Hope sustains us through experiences we never imagined we'd encounter along the way.

One of my dearest friends from Zambia is a lady named Princess Kasune Zulu whose life story is truly remarkable. Her autobiography entitled *Warrior Princess* is a highly recommended read! She saw both of her parents die from AIDS when she was barely a teenager and as the oldest child, she dropped out of school and took care of her siblings while watching her parents die in their home. She married a much older man while still in her teens in order to provide food and shelter for her younger siblings and contracted the HIV virus from him. She had two girls herself at a rather young age and had every reason to be bitter at God and withdraw into a life of rebellion or depression or disillusionment concerning the world. However, she was a lady who somehow, someway latched onto the hope of a God who overcomes and is with us in the midst of great pain and challenge. She decided she would devote her life to the education and prevention of HIV/AIDS even as she lived with the disease herself.

Her voice was full of hope and her clear and compelling message took her to radio shows in Zambia and eventually to speaking all across the United States and the world about the needs in Africa. We had her speak at our school several times and she was one of the most engaging and energetic communicators ever to step on our chapel stage. She became a dear friend and our family celebrated with her as she remarried in Chicago many years after that first marriage in Zambia so long ago. Her daughters, Joy and Faith, have enrolled as students at Wheaton Academy and Princess Zulu is a full-fledged Wheaton Academy mom. She could have never imagined the life she would go through and we would have never imagined that we would have girls from Zambia before our school got involved in responding to the AIDS pandemic. Yet the hope found in the love and protection and care of Jesus has sustained her life and brought to our community girls whose constant smiles and warm shouts of greeting to me across the hallway have cemented my trust and hope that God can do anything and surprises us along the journey in such unlikely and beautiful ways.

It's OK to ask God for a miracle...because He's a God who makes the impossible become reality.

I've often felt conflicted about asking God to do the supernatural almost as if I am asking Him to do something that will make Him stretch and get out of His comfort zone in order to answer my plea. Life in my world is so ordered, so scheduled, so managed, and so accomplished that my need and perhaps even my want for a divine, unexplainable act of the powerful hand of the Creator of the universe is limited and viewed as unnecessary.

In Kakolo Village, the members of the community began praying that somehow, someway God would bring a school, their very first school, to their little home because they knew that the education of their children was absolutely essential in helping them to have a different life than the one they were experiencing. They prayed for nearly two years, not knowing how it would happen, not asking the government for resources, not doing anything beyond trusting that God could in His sovereignty and power bring a new school to an empty dirt field. And instead of having taxpayers approve higher taxes to finance a construction project, God did something a bit more radical and sent His Spirit into the hearts of a bunch of rich high school kids in a suburb in the heartland of the United States. I mean really, who could ever even dream up the craziest of notions that a bunch of kids on the other side of the planet would be the answer to their prayers of great faith? God's miraculous, stupendous ways included making the impossible reality through the most unconventional of ways. Almost every day, I still am dumbstruck that our high school is so deeply connected with this place so far away, so different, so hidden from our eyes. Only a God who is in the business of supernatural, irrational, and brilliant workings could make prayers answered, schools appear, and lives changed through this most extraordinary example of what He is capable of and longs to do in our world with so many needs. I think I can now finally get myself to ask for God to intervene and show up in unexpected ways and places in my own life these days because I see Him doing miracles in Africa every day.

PLAYING BASEBALL AND EATING DINNER WITH MY SPONSORED CHILD IN ZAMBIA

Greg Steinsdoerfer

Between my junior and senior year in college I spent ten weeks serving as an intern with World Vision Zambia while living with the people of Kakolo Village. It was obviously a time like none other for me, and two memories stand out from a summer that changed my life.

One of the most memorable and remarkable parts of my living in Kakolo Village was that the child I had sponsored through World Vision lived less than a ten-minute walk from my house. During this trip I was able to not only experience the joy of meeting him, but eating dinner and hanging out with him on a daily basis. My sponsored child's name is Zangata. At the time I met him he was twelve years old, and like many children in sub-Saharan Africa he is an orphan. His father passed away when he was seven and he lived with his mom and all his brothers and sisters. Zangata is the youngest in his family; he is quiet and yet is one of the most determined kids I have ever met. He is shy around people he doesn't know, but has a surprising confidence at times when he is with his friends. I remember the exact moment when I met Zangata (Za for short) for the first time. My roommate, Samson, who also works for World Vision, walked me over to Za's house on a Sunday afternoon shortly after I arrived in Kakolo. Za was sitting in his house talking with a few of his friends. After greeting and talking to him for a few minutes I asked if I could meet the rest of his family and was introduced to his sister and brother-in-law. I asked through my translator if I could meet his mom, only to find out that she had passed away just a month ago. Deep sadness came over me with the realization that my sponsored child was now what we called a double orphan (both parents deceased). I could see the hurt and pain in his eyes even though we could have little verbal communication at the time. I knew that this child had been through more pain in his twelve years of life than I may ever know in my lifetime. And although he tried to hide the pain, it was unmistakably there. As most sponsors do when they meet their child, I brought him a gift, a brand-new soccer ball. As I gave it to him I couldn't help but feel somewhat inadequate. Here I am giving him a soccer ball; is that really supposed to make him feel better about not having any parents? It seemed to help for the first initial moments, at least. Za loved that soccer ball and never let it out of his sight; in fact, many of the other boys in the village also learned to love that single soccer ball.

It became one of my top priorities to learn about his life and who he was as a person, and to then encourage him about his future. Every night it became routine for Za and a friend to come over for dinner with my room-mates and I. Zambian meals are a lot different than what I was accustomed to eating. Rural Zambians often eat one meal a day, occasionally mixing in a light snack. These meals always consist of nshima which is ground up corn, made into a mush type texture that has not a hint of flavor. If the family can afford it, they eat nshima with a side item, most often a type of green vegetable or sweet potato. And maybe once a year at special occasions, meat appears!

It was through our dinner conversations that I was able to understand Za and his thoughts, his plans, his dreams, and his pains. Za loved to play soccer, and he was a talented athlete. He was big for his age which gave him a slight advantage over the others. He didn't have a favorite professional player because they don't have TVs in Kakolo, and even radios are still quite rare. Like most children in Zambia, Za loved school and scored particularly well in math and science. His English skills were poor compared to others in his class, and he shared with me that he dreamed of becoming a medical doctor one day. It was hard for me to think that the realistic odds of him becoming a doctor were slim to none, and I tried my best to inspire him to follow his dreams. It was my dream to come here, and I never thought it would be possible. It is actually possible that he might someday become a doctor. A lot of the other kids in the village dreamed of being a professional soccer player, or teacher, or taxi driver, even though most of these children have never been in a car, stepped foot on a university campus, or watched a professional soccer match.

After we finished eating, our house would often fill with other boys who would come to hang out, talk, and play games late into the night. I remember buying a deck of cards in town for about a dollar and teaching the kids new card games. A deck of playing cards was a luxury and few, if any, of the children had ever played with them before. I was told by my roommates that the children talked about playing these games most of the day and couldn't stop describing what they had experienced with everyone they knew. The bond I was able to form with Za was an incredible experience, more than I could ever have imagined, and something that I will never forget.

As I was packing my bag to spend that summer in Zambia I found myself looking at a baseball sitting on my desk. I remember thinking, "What's the point of bringing a baseball? Nobody in Zambia would know or even care how to play." I remembered from my previous visit that people in Zambia loved learning about life in America. Baseball has always been a huge part of my life. I've been playing the game since I was old enough to walk. So I stuffed that baseball at the bottom of my suitcase and didn't think much about it.

No one in Kakolo had ever heard of baseball. Futball (American soccer) is literally the only sport in this village. For weeks that baseball sat at the bottom of my bag as I played countless hours of soccer in the community.

One of the drawbacks to being an American is that I am used to being and staying busy. As exciting as it was to live in Kakolo, there were plenty of moments on long weekends when time seemed to stand still. On these long weekends I was left entirely on my own in terms of the challenge of trying to speak in Bemba. On one particularly long Saturday, I remember finding that baseball and pulling it out of my bag. I walked over to my roommate and tossed the ball at him. He looked at it and asked me what it was. I asked if he would like to hear about my favorite sport, to which he quickly agreed. I began to describe the game of baseball as best I could. It was quite the task, as there are so many complicated phrases and words that baseball uses that simply do not translate very easily into an African language. It took over an hour to explain the game, and afterwards we went outside and played "catch." We played with no gloves or anything else that would alleviate the pain of a hard throw. We spent a lot of time laughing, and it actually took us most of a day to go through the basics of how to play catch.

By late afternoon my roommate was ready to put these new skills into action. He gathered a group of kids (always an easy thing to do). We set up a field in the village using what we could find: rocks for bases, and a rusty old metal pipe for a bat. It was hysterical watching them attempt to learn to play the game. I don't think in all my years of playing baseball I had ever enjoyed it more. The game began mostly with confusion and chaos, which was followed by more laughter and excitement as the players began to understand a new game. The game progressed slowly as everything, and I mean everything, needed to be explained over and over again. We continued to play in what seemed to me to be a dream. Baseball does not end at the sound of a whistle, but continues until the game is completed. For us, the game continued until the sun dipped well below the horizon. When all light had faded, I deemed it was necessary to suspend the game due to the dangerous nature of playing in the dark with hard objects.

The next day kids were lining up to play more baseball. The games became more competitive as a few of the players actually understood some parts of the game and developed their own unique playing style. Some players got really good at bunting down the first baseline, while others developed a method of stopping the ball with their feet and picking it up quickly. The rock bases turned into plastic bags, and several of the kids spent the early morning hours cutting down tree limbs to use as bats in the game. The second game was just as chaotic and fun as the first game.

I was so excited about the games that when I made it to the office I e-mailed my friends and family describing the games we had just played. A friend of mine at World Vision, Tony Frank, received one of these e-mails and forwarded it on to an old friend at ESPN who worked alongside a well-known sportswriter, Jim Caple. Jim sent me an e-mail asking for more details about the game and the whole baseball in Zambia experience. A few days later he published an article that was read all over the world. My inbox was flooded with dozens of e-mails from people who had read the story and now wanted to help these kids in Kakolo. The response to the story was overwhelming to me. I could hardly contain my excitement. I ran around the office showing everyone the story and the e-mail responses that were coming from Europe, Japan, and both coasts of the US. The responses turned into a new project that continued to pick up momentum, and literally a few weeks later our office in Kitwe began receiving the first shipments of baseball equipment to be used at our first real practices.

While the baseball gear was coming in the mail, a few World Vision staff members and I went through the process of setting up a baseball league. We recruited coaches and educated them the best we could on the rules of the game, and they in turn recruited enough kids to make several teams. We set up a league schedule and a budget which even included travel expenses for teams to go from one area to another. The children, coaches, and community began to really understand the game of baseball and I got to see two of my biggest passions play out together before me: the people of Zambia and the game of baseball. Two of my passions that I never would have dreamed would be connected were brought together through the genius of our Creator. Throughout the rest of my trip I enjoyed our games and loved watching the kids begin to master the very complex game of baseball. It also brought full circle something that God had been trying to teach me for the last few years: God is willing to work miracles in the lives of those who are open to the leadings of His Spirit.

Initially when I came back to the States after my summer in Africa, people often asked me, "How was your trip?" I'm not sure if I ever came up with a sufficient answer to that question; there are just some things that can't be put into words. I know that I came back a completely different person with an entirely new perspective on life; I simply will never be the same again. I have daily reminders of the blessings in my life that many other people across the world don't get to experience. When I come home to a dark house I just reach for a light switch, and years later I still marvel at how I do not have to stumble around looking for matches and a candle to provide light. Each time I take a shower I feel so blessed that I don't have to stand in a dark room with a cold bucket of water to rinse myself clean. I am reminded of how amazing it is to twist a knob and get hot water. When people complain about how tasteless their food is, I think back to eating the most bland meal of nshima for weeks on end. I sometimes fight the urge to say phrases like, "You have no idea what bland really is!" When I find myself getting anxious over being a few minutes late to work, I remind myself that people in Kakolo have anxiety over where their next meal is going to come from. There are moments when I find myself getting upset that I have to pay a hundred dollars to replace a flat tire that only a few hours before had been perfectly fine. Then I think back to my family in Kakolo, most of whom have never ridden in a car. The thought of actually being able to drive a car would be a lifetime achievement! Even sharing one village car to take people to and from health clinics and for emergencies is too much of a financial burden for the village to bear. I still laugh at the thought that I had to climb a large anthill in the village to get reception to use my cell phone.

These surface level changes still affect me on a daily basis, but living in Kakolo also reshaped my heart and the core of who I am. Growing up as a product of the suburbs, I had never learned how to live in complete dependence on the God who created the universe. When all your physical and emotional needs are met, it is difficult to learn how to do this. Living in an environment where I did not speak the language, I often just felt alone. It forced me to depend on a God who promised to never leave me, and we began a new and deeper relationship. In the midst of feeling alone I felt a stronger love and companionship than I had ever felt before.

These were things that the center place of Christian America had failed to teach me. It was something that six years of Christian education never included in its curriculum. And here it was, right in front of me. The people in Kakolo also taught me what it looks like to live with joy. The people of Kakolo face unspeakable hardships and pain each day. It was from them that I learned what true joy looks like, that deep sense of joy that fills a life and spills over to other's lives. I learned that true joy, true contentment does not come from where you live, but how you live. And these lessons will stay with me for a lifetime.

In the summer of 2011, five years after I spent two-and-a-half months in Zambia I returned with my wife to visit Kakolo and to catch up with old friends. It was an incredible experience to return and see almost a decade of progress from when I had first been introduced to the community of Kakolo. One question that I am often asked is, "Can Americans really help make a difference in the lives of those in sub-Saharan Africa?" I think they are essentially wondering if their time and resources might actually be wasted. I can without any doubts say, "Yes, lives can change!" I have seen an entire community transformed through the help of many Americans. Kids are getting a better education, hunger is decreasing, lives are being saved by better health care, and the church is taking a leading role in the community in caring for the sick and destitute. The change was so drastic that it didn't even feel like the same place.

Greg is currently enrolled in a PhD program in counseling psychology at Southern Illinois University. He has served as program supervisor at a hospital psychiatric unit and would love to teach in Africa someday.

CHAPTER 7

READING THE SCRIPTURES WITH NEW EYES

Religion that God our Father accepts as pure and faultless is this: to look after orphans and widows in their distress (James 1:27).[20]

When I was in junior high, I began to practice the daily habit of a "quiet time" after being challenged to do so by a small group leader in my youth group. I owned a small red NIV bible that had my initials along with a cross that had been burned on the cover by one of the other youth staff at our church. I read almost the whole New Testament over the next few years. For some reason, I decided that I should underline any verse I found to be meaningful in my look at the text each day. I soon had underlined thousands of verses, and as the years passed, began to write comments into the margins as I heard specific passages preached on in various church settings.

I still own that small red Bible, and it is the one I take when I go backpacking in the mountains or on other trips when I want to bring a copy of the Scriptures that doesn't take up much physical space. In a tangible way, it represents the reality that I was raised in a evangelical world that convinced me the Bible was clearly and undoubtedly the guiding force in the growth and development and basis of my faith in Jesus. It really did dictate the manner in which I was seeking to live my life as a serious Christian. And even now as I have served as the head of a Christian high school Bible department and have spent most of my professional life daily seeking to teach and make the Bible relevant and come alive for a generation of students, I am unbelievably grateful that the Word of God has and continues to hold a place of priority in my life, in many ways due to the early years where I read, studied, discussed, underlined, and listened to its life-giving words.

However, several years ago I began to wrestle with questions that continue to shake me up and cause me to be even more intentional about reading and knowing all that is in this amazing book. The questions were, "Had I read and studied and listened to sermons for most of my life and yet not really seen, heard, and embraced some of the major ideas and themes that were written about all throughout the Bible? Did my basic biblical theology have a huge hole in it despite all the time I had devoted to trying to get to know God's nature and plan for His people and the world?" In some ways, I wanted to just remain fixed securely with my paradigm I had created and adopted about what the Scriptures presented as sufficient, but I soon became more and more convinced that I had to find the answer to these probing questions. For if I truly believed that each part, each book in the Bible was inspired and important, it was my duty, my calling to make sure that I tried even in my mental shortcomings to unearth all the truth and principles and stories found within its writings.

One of the latest Bibles I've received in the mail is one quite different from that little red one in some ways, and yet contains the very same words and truth inside its covers. This recently published Bible came from the British and Foreign Bible Society, titled *The Poverty and Justice Bible*. The title obviously speaks to the publisher's desire to highlight these issues of poverty and justice as ones that are prominent and must be noticed when one reads, studies, interprets, and applies the Bible as a follower of Jesus. When I saw the title, I chuckled a bit because the reality is that for the first twenty to twenty-five years that I spent as a reader and student of the Bible, those two concepts were pretty much absent from what I saw and accordingly talked about when it came to what I believed was inside the pages of Scripture.

Somehow, someway those themes so present in the Bible were essentially invisible to me as a reader and teacher of the Word of God. I can't remember hearing a specific sermon growing up or in my early days of ministry specifically addressing these topics from the pulpit in the myriad of churches I attended. I know that I read hundreds, if not thousands of these verses that deal with God's care for the poor and His unending passion for justice, and it is almost a certainty that I was distracted or not listening when speakers I heard addressed these topics. But I am sure of this: I was immersed in Christian education and evangelical church culture for the better part of two decades, and yet did not come away with a personal theology holding as a key idea that God was incredibly interested in how His people thought about and lived when it came to the condition of the billions of people in the world He created who were poor, sick, and oppressed. I am still to this day disappointed that I failed to read the Bible with open eyes, and am actually incredulous that the church of Jesus Christ I was so deeply a part of did not speak to these issues with any sort of clarity, strength, or frequency. It remains a mystery to me how this happened based on the vast amount of biblical teaching encounters and experiences present in my faith journey.

As I began to page through this newest Bible in my collection, I immediately noticed something that looked very familiar, but in reality was something I had never seen before. The Bible had thousands of verses highlighted in orange. As I made the pages go quickly through my fingers, I saw this somewhat obnoxious color on what seemed like nearly every page in the whole 1,234 pages of this particular paperback Bible. As I'm sure you have guessed, the editors of the Bible society group went through the whole text of the Bible and then highlighted in orange during its printing almost three thousand different verses that speak directly to the issues of poverty and justice. I have now heard church leaders like Bill Hybels and Rick Warren and even our past two US presidents speak over and over about the thousands of verses in Scripture that mention the poor. However, seeing this bright orange color all over its pages was a powerful visual picture of the evidence on almost every page of how deeply and passionately God cares about these issues of poverty and justice.

A few years ago some of my students heard me mention this idea that there were thousands of references made concerning God's passion for the care of the poor and oppressed in Scripture, and they came up with the idea that we needed to try and somehow communicate this reality to our student body that still struggled at times with the notion that being involved in "social justice work" was truly a biblical thing to do. After brainstorming about what we could do to try to show the volume of verses that endorsed caring for the needs of those suffering around the world, they decided to grab a big, long roll of paper and write out all the verses that they could find that talked about God's love and concern for the poor.

After just a cursory look at the massive amount of words in Scripture addressing this topic, they figured they would have to skip doing their homework for a few weeks if they wrote them all out word for word, and instead decided to just write out the references for this collection of verses. They started writing them out on this roll of yellow paper, and soon found that after finishing maybe ten percent of the list they had compiled from looking at Bible concordances, they had already created a sheet that was a couple of feet high and stretched at least forty feet all the way across our auditorium stage.

They unrolled this scroll of sorts during our annual Zambia Project opening chapel, and as it extended out further and further across our large platform in front of the student body it was a powerfully effective picture of the vastness of God's interest in seeing the needs of the least in our world taken seriously.

As I have read many of these verses and examined what they mean for how I am to live differently as a Christian who wants to have his life reflect what the Scriptures value as significant in God's eyes, four major biblical concepts have emerged as foundational in being the guideposts for our work in Zambia over the past several years:

Compassion: God's heart is bent powerfully toward and beats for those in need!

In the Gospels, the compassion of Jesus is nothing less than extraordinary, especially when one considers the place of moral authority and spiritual power He occupied in relationship to others. The needs of the people whom Jesus both knew and even just ran into during His travels almost always demanded from him both attention and response. This simple statement in Matthew's Gospel is one of the clearest summaries when it records Jesus' actions this way:

"When Jesus landed and saw a large crowd, he had compassion on them and healed their sick" (Matthew 14:14).[21]

One of the things about the compassion and many responses of physical healing demonstrated by Jesus is that He was not asking people how they had gotten sick; this was so countercultural in a religious system that often connected the dots between the sins present in people's lives and the deserved punishment from God both in the present day and for the generations that followed someone's moral misgivings. The kind of compassion that spilled out of Jesus daily was that which focused on the need rather than only the causes of one's condition.

I have found something else in my own personal integration of compassion into my heart and life. As I was literally broken on our Zambia trips at the sight of orphans, moms, and dads just like me dying in their huts as their children watched, and the incredible struggle for daily survival, I found myself changed beyond an emotional experience written about on my daily blog for readers at home. To this day, I can literally begin to cry at any point when I talk about Africa or even see a film highlighting the needs I have shown multiple times to groups. I now almost always give money to people who ask for it on the streets in my own community and my heart is pretty much a jumbled mess, where I feel like I can't control and maintain the same emotional stability that once was a hallmark of my adult male life. Deep in my soul I feel like I am different because I have met God in an unexpected way and in unexpected places. That is why I am a different person on most days than I was before I read about and saw in practice the compassionate heart of the One whose life example I must pursue. This quote from a famous musician reflects my experience as I've run smack into the compassion of my Savior and Lord.

> God is in the slums, in the cardboard boxes where the poor
>   play house.
> God is in the silence of a mother who has infected her child
> with a virus that will end both their lives.
> God is in the cries heard under the rubble of war.
> God is in the debris of wasted opportunity and lives, and
> God is with us if we are with them.
>   BONO[22]

I used to see compassion as something I should pursue in order to help bring the love of Christ to people in a tangible way. However, it may be even more than that. It may be that when we choose to not meet the needs of others, we actually pull away the presence and power of God. The connection between the compassion of God's people and the love of God is so deep, so strong, that we can even damage or perhaps cast aside the love of God that is evident and felt in our world when we choose to ignore the pull of God's Spirit on our hearts to be people of compassion. Eugene Peterson states it this way in his paraphrase of a familiar passage:

If you see some brother or sister in need and have the means to do something about it but turn a cold shoulder and do nothing, what happens to God's love? It disappears. And you made it disappear (1 John 3:17).[23]

Justice: We are blessed to bless others, especially those in great need!

We live in a time when so many people are yearning to see justice done in a world where extreme poverty shortens the lives of millions each year. Grassroots movements opposing practices such as child soldiers, forced prostitution, and modern-day slavery have gained incredible traction in the church and the larger culture. I have shown my students films like Invisible Children, Glue Boys, Call + Response, and Blood Diamond, and they have drawn immediate and deep response from the "next" generation. My college students want to do their internships with organizations like International Justice Mission and World Vision that are on the front lines of attempting to deal with the legal and political justice issues demanding a response around the globe. The Bible obviously speaks loudly about justice, but selective hearing and reading has often masked the volume and depth of these passages in God's Word for many of us. A verse I sang through my own youth group and college days has taken on new meaning and significance as I identify the priority of living out the nature of a just God in the way we function as a church and how we persuade our culture to act when injustice is so clearly evident:

> *He has shown you, O mortal, what is good. And what does the LORD require of you? To act justly and to love mercy and to walk humbly with your God. (Micah 6:8)[24]*

Justice in the Scriptures also involves more than just speaking out when we see things that are wrong, and then seeking to discover opportunities to exert political leverage that can help to make things right. The movement from a corporate level to a personal level takes justice to the place in our lives where it truly becomes a facet of our character.

One of the most compelling and longest-lasting lessons of our involvement in Zambia is the simple reality that our work there isn't something radical, but in fact it is actually what God designed us to be doing all along, especially in light of how first-century church life is described in the first few chapters of the book of Acts. There has been and continues to be an entitlement mind-set present in our culture and our churches that when I have worked to make good money, I am then allowed to spend and enjoy for myself because I have earned it. As you see the lives and worlds of others around the globe and even just outside our own backyards, you begin to realize that our hard work has also been mixed often with incredible economic opportunity and advantage in comparison to what is reality for people just like us in other communities and places outside of the world of privilege where we have always resided.

It is almost impossible to not ask questions after a visit to places like Kakolo Village about why God chose to allow me to be born in a city like Dallas, Texas, instead of Kitwe, Zambia. Those questions can seem to have no real answer, but I have come to believe that there is one answer that makes the most sense as I grapple with this seeming injustice that begins with one's birthplace. Because of where I live and the incredible opportunities God has given me to gain remarkable amounts of resource through my work in comparison to my sisters and brothers around the world, I am one of the preferred solutions in God's eyes as He sees the needs of those He loves all over the globe.

My blessings are not so I can enjoy anything and everything I see and want and think I need. My blessing is given to help answer that most difficult question of why I am so privileged in comparison to so many on this planet. Pointing out that the money spent on Black Friday in the United States could provide clean water for everyone in the world who needs it should not be just a guilt-inducing statement. Instead, such examples should promote questions I ought to be asking myself every day I make a purchase as a consumer.

The calling to be a tangible blessing that gives hope and life as one who is blessed is a lifetime justice mandate. Solomon expresses it perfectly in this verse:

> *"Do not withhold good from those who deserve it when it's in your power to help them" (Proverbs 3:27).*[25]

Our job is, then, to be advocates and distributors of justice wherever things simply are not right—here, there, and everywhere. God longs to connect us as a global church when we respond to injustices. All those in need don't just need our help, but instead they deserve it, and we have the power to help them, even more so as we join together with others who have been blessed to be a blessing. And as we become conduits of blessing we model for the watching world the very nature of our great God.

Imago Dei: We are compelled to treat each of our neighbors in the world as ones who bear the image of God and for whom Christ chose to die.

The Bible begins in the very first chapter by lifting up one of the most significant doctrines found in all of Scripture: the reality that as human beings we were stamped undoubtedly in the amazing creative process of our God with His very nature and characteristics. Each one born, whether healthy or terminally ill, whether athletic or unable to move, whether a brilliant thinker or only able to process at the simplest of levels, whether beautiful or scarred, reflects the very image of the indescribable Lord and Creator and Ruler and Savior of all. This verse changes how we ought to view everyone we interact with in our globalized world:

> *God created mankind in his own image, in the image of God he created them; male and female he created them....God blessed them and said to them, "Be fruitful and increase in number; fill the earth and subdue it"....God saw all that he had made, and it was very good. (Genesis 1:27, 28, 31)*[26]

The moral implications of the doctrine of Imago Dei are apparent in the fact that if humans are created in God's very image, then humans must begin to actually view and treat one another as if they have value, significance, and great worth. This reality means everything as we consider what it means to be a witness to the gospel, an obedient reader of all of Scripture, a follower of Jesus, and a human being who views and treats people with Genesis 1:27 eyes despite what appears before us.

We used this quote as the backdrop for one of our school fine arts festivals responding to the issues of justice and equality. It speaks to the importance of seeing what happens to those who have both very little and very much in relationship to this stamp God imparted at creation:

> *Of this we can be sure, that poverty...mars the image of*
> *God within humanity; it mars the image of God in the*
> *poor, the sick, the oppressed, the least as it deprives them of*
> *opportunities for abundant life. It mars the image of God*
> *within those of us who have more than enough, but who*
> *through greed, complacency or even ignorance fail to do the*
> *justice to embrace the loving kindness that our God asks of us.*
> *Njongonkulu Ndungane,*
> *Archbishop of Cape Town, South Africa*[27]

It is indeed our privilege, our calling, our job in this day to be the people of Jesus who reverse that marring of the image of God both for the poor, the sick, and the oppressed, and then for the greedy, complacent, and ignorant as we are the expression of God's highest value of all those who need to have God's image restored to its full beauty in their lives.

Cultural Engagement...faith in action: we are called to bring the Kingdom to this world.

I have prayed the Lord's prayer out loud well over a thousand times in my life. I went to a Presbyterian church for much of my growing up years and repeated it every Sunday. I have prayed it with large groups in massive auditoriums and with small gatherings on the top of isolated mountains. The words are ingrained into my consciousness in a way that few things are, except for maybe some catchphrases from movies or SportsCenter anchors.

However, as is often the case, when words are repeated they can easily be said without examining what one is really saying. I prayed the following phrase so many times without a thought about the radical meaning it had for what I would do each day if I believed its words to be literally true:

"Your kingdom come, your will be done, on earth as it is in heaven" (Matthew 6:10).[28]

As I began to break down this one sentence, I was struck by what I had never really seen or heard in the prayer Jesus taught His disciples to pray. I only focused on the last word rather than the four two-letter words before it in this sentence. I lived like I believed that the Kingdom was only to come when we would go to heaven one day. That mind-set caused me to be deeply apathetic about the need to make the Kingdom of God Jesus announced He had come to bring visible in my lifetime. As I began to read the ways Jesus talked about this vitally central concept of the Kingdom and the apostle Paul continued to write about in his Epistles, it became another stake in my framework of the key truths that attached together made up my expanding biblical worldview. And this simple notion changed everything in terms of what I knew I needed to do when going out to the world after praying the Lord's Prayer: The Kingdom of God is both a future event and a present reality.

I found incredible teaching about this notion of the Kingdom in the spoken and written words of British theologian N.T. Wright as he reflected on verses like this passage Paul penned:

God was pleased to have all his fullness dwell in him, and through him to reconcile to himself all things, whether things on earth or things in heaven, by making peace through his blood, shed on the cross. (Colossians 1:19-20)[29]

Wright in his commentary on Colossians discusses how the supremacy of Christ manifests itself and demonstrates remarkable ability to bring the Kingdom of God through the Lordship of His Son to all peoples and all places and all things in this incredible section of Scripture in Colossians:

> *There is no sphere of existence over which Jesus is not sovereign, in virtue of his role both in creation (1:16-17) and in reconciliation (1:18-20). There can be no dualistic division between some areas which he rules and others which he does not. "There is no neutral ground in the universe: every square inch, every split second, is claimed by God and counterclaimed by Satan." The task of evangelism is therefore best understood as the proclamation that Jesus is already Lord, that in him God's new creation has broken into history, and that all people are therefore summoned to submit to him in love, worship, and obedience. The logic of this message requires that those who announce it should be seeking to bring Christ's Lordship to bear on every area of human and worldly existence. Christians must work to help create conditions in which human beings, and the whole created world, can live as God always intended.[30]*

The good news—the great news—of the coming of the Kingdom is for the whole person. Physically one can receive healing, intellectually one's mind can be transformed through the teaching of the Scriptures, and spiritually one's heart and soul are changed. They are changed into ones that care and love deeply that which Jesus Himself made and loved enough to go to the cross to bring full restoration to—that which was indeed eternally marred and broken. I've tended to only emphasize the spiritual exchange that takes place when Christ wants everything about us to become more like Him. Jesus Christ has come so that the Kingdom of God can invade our world, our cultures, our lives; and may we both pray and join the Spirit of God at work in our world today in helping the Kingdom to be released and to come in all its glory and power and impact.

A couple of summers ago our family had our first experience at Disney World in Orlando, Florida. Going there truly is an overwhelming and exhilarating experience, especially when you've been in a Zambian village the month before. We had a great time and our kids absolutely loved being in the Magic Kingdom theme park. Our favorite "ride" was actually an interactive movie theater experience called *Mickey's PhilharMagic* where you sit in your seat and watch all the familiar characters and songs and scenes from several different Disney movies go through an adventure on the huge screen in front of you. I found out that you can actually watch several different taped versions of the short film on YouTube at any moment. However, watching it at home is missing the one thing that makes it the ride you'll stand in line for and go back to several times during the day at Disney World. When you walk into the theater, you pick up a pair of yellow glasses that cause the next ten minutes to become three-dimensional instead of the usual two dimensions in a movie watching experience. My four-year-old son actually kept falling off his seat to grab the items and characters that appeared to literally be coming toward us in our seats. Disney mixes in actual water spray and the smell of cinnamon to transport you to the place where you find yourself completely engaged in all your senses with the events unfolding on the big screen. I was amazed even as an adult at the power of the full 3-D experience to entertain and captivate you in ways that watching a regular movie never could if you watched just the film on a screen or monitor.

In a strangely comparable way, I have felt like I put on a different set of glasses to read Scripture over the last several years as I have seen the full narrative present in the Bible come alive right before my very eyes. I always have believed that the Scriptures are good and worth my attention. Only in the last decade or so would I honestly tell you that the Word of God has become multidimensional for me. It has truly called and moved me to see the world and its people with the clarity and compassion and sense of their reality that God's writings are designed to give to us as His instruments of reconciliation and redemption.

The biblical teachings on God's concern for the poor and His desire for justice have jumped off the pages. They've caused me to see what needs are truly present all over the planet. They have compelled me to reach out of my seat and bring food and water and medicine and shelter and the Scriptures themselves in Jesus' name. I am one who cannot sit and just watch the world from my comfortable, cushioned seat. The gospel has become so real and compelling that the theology present in its story has caused me to become captured by the mission of God in my intellectual, emotional, physical, and spiritual senses. And the lives of the people that God loves so deeply, has designed as His finest creation bearing His image, and sent Jesus to provide forgiveness for have finally become the priority in my life and ministry in full and living color.

I recently found that little red Bible as I prepared to move some books to my new office. I even found some of the passages I have listed in this chapter underlined, most likely being marked up during my high school and college years. My prayer has been and continues to be for myself and all those in the church both now and in the future that we would not read the Scriptures with eyes only half open, unable to see all that is written concerning the advance of God's Kingdom and the complete transformation His love is designed to have upon each and every person's life. Reading this one book with my eyes wide open has altered how I think and live on every level every day and in every way. I am closing this chapter with a final quote that speaks to my own new discoveries as a Bible-believing follower of Jesus Christ from the back cover of the new Bible I am reading from these days. Rob Bell, as quoted in *The Poverty and Justice Bible*[31] says:

The real danger in our world may not be people failing to read the Bible—it may be what happens when people actually do read it—especially the over 2000 verses on God's heart for the poor and oppressed. Be warned...the pages of Scripture can change everything.[32]

RESPONSIBILITY

Laura Finch

Responsibility. Just reading the word may make you wilt a little bit. Doesn't it make you think of paying your taxes, not being crazy when you'd like to be, and coming to a complete stop at stop signs? As a high school junior it made me groan because it meant band practice logs and obeying curfew. It was a nagging word I thought applied mostly to me and my personal habits, and I'm sure I never imagined that it could play into my calling. Not that it was a foreign concept; my parents, who have adopted once and taken in foster kids many times, run a tight ship. They're pretty much experts in responsibility: obey the house rules, honor your school commitments, and put your birthday checks in the bank. But as it turns out, being responsible isn't actually as personal, nor as conservative a concept as I used to think.

My understanding of responsibility really started to change while sitting on my bed reading *Rich Christians in an Age of Hunger*. Absorbing the statistics (go to globalrichlist.com to get the idea) and then realizing what percentage of the Bible actually is devoted to verses about the poor and about finances floored me. "For such a time as this, you were placed upon the earth." "Freely you have received, freely give." "All that we have accomplished, you have done for us." All the verses that had impacted me so profoundly my senior year in high school came flooding back, like a levee bursting and wiping any preconceived notions about my calling off the map. I thought about Wheaton and its affluence. I thought about the US and its relation to the rest of the world on the pay scale. I thought about legacies, and having this one short century to live and make a mark in a hurting world. I thought about how on a stormy Halloween night in the early eighties when no one even knew that AIDS was an acronym for something, I was born into this privileged, responsible family that was already setting aside money for my education. What was I going to do with these great gifts of life and health? They weren't mine. If the harvest is ready, why not...harvest? There was a whole new realm of possibility opening up, not just the possibility that maybe my choice of career didn't have to be based on the probable salary, but the possibility of going into decision-making and decision-influencing full time: that big, scary, controversial, hated world of politics.

Up to this point I hated pretty much everything about politics. I especially disliked the skinny white boys in my classes who had read all the World War II books and thought they knew everything about everything. The story of how I ended up marrying one of these boys is for some other book, but the point is that I was turned off by everything about politics, as many Christians are. The whole process was corrupt, far off, and frankly pretty boring.

However, one afternoon in 2003 I was sure the answer was to make sure the US paid their fair share. Although we gave, at that time, a higher dollar amount than any other country to foreign aid, we still gave the smallest percentage of our GDP. To me, that seemed like the ultimate example of selfishness and apathy. I didn't know what was being done about AIDS on a large scale, but I wanted to know.

See, the crazy thing about high school is that when you start you've just left childhood, and when you finish you're supposed to be ready to choose a career. Maybe I tuned out during some chapel talk, or maybe I missed some elective class I should have taken, or maybe I had been ignoring it all just because it sounded too "responsible." But I don't remember anybody explaining to me what an interest group was, what grassroots fundraising was, or what it took to influence the political process or the effect it can have. I'm ashamed to say that I hadn't really made the connection that "organizations" are actually just groups of people who all care about one thing as they are organized together. Maybe the Zambia Project was just the first thing that finally awakened me to the outside world, but I wanted answers. I wanted to know what this "activism" looked like. How could the epidemic be stopped? Where should the money come from and where was it coming from currently? Would time be better spent fundraising in the private sector, that huge, fat, sleeping giant called the Church, or trying to convince the government of the most powerful nation in the world to spend more money outside of itself?

I entered my freshman year at Taylor University still unsure of my role in the whole thing. Within Taylor's ministry umbrella, known as Taylor World Outreach (TWO), I found friends who were just as dismayed at the state of our world, and just as open to be a part of the work God was doing. They didn't claim to have all the answers, but they were aware of what was going on, and simply put, they got it. I was drawn to people like my dear friend Valerie, who has a passion for all things having to do with social justice and is a Peace Corps volunteer in China at this very moment; Andrew, who agreed with me that it was ridiculous for Taylor not to have an organization addressing AIDS issues, and who is now in law school; and Val and Margie, who were always the ones behind the scenes orchestrating Taylor's missions events, and who are now studying in seminary and ministering in Jordan, respectively. I started researching other human rights issues and was excited to find that a relationship between Taylor and World Vision had already begun and that its brand-new college arm, Acting on AIDS, would help us plant a chapter on our campus.

I threw myself into Acting on AIDS fundraisers and educational events and loved every minute of it. And on May 24, 2005, I wrote this in my prayer journal: "God, I was a nobody, and still am. But use me anyway! Use me to unite Christian colleges across America, even if just behind the scenes." Ironically that prayer was answered in February 2006, during my junior year, when World Vision chose to hold the first Acting on AIDS Summit Conference at Taylor. Students from all around came to stay on Taylor's campus. Together we attended workshops and seminars, and met people like Princess Zulu, a World Vision spokeswoman who also happened to be Zambian. There could not have been a better culmination to our efforts, and

I was overjoyed that the work begun at my high school was translating to my college peers as well.

While I was looking forward to the future, I didn't want to be Activist Annie at college and then forget everything as soon as I graduated. I knew I wanted the Zambia Project to be a way of life for me, and I felt strongly that it would play into my calling, and wanted to spend a semester away from campus in a place that would help make that calling clearer. I toyed with the idea of studying in Uganda for a semester, and ultimately decided that having already been to Zambia for one life-changing trip in 2004, I didn't need to be convinced that God was working in Africa and I wanted to be a part of it. I decided instead to study for three months in Washington, DC, and to intern with the ONE Campaign, a coalition of many reputable NGOs who all cared about one thing: ending poverty.

Living in DC and working at ONE confirmed I was on the right track. I met, lived with, and studied with even more students and teachers who were on the same page I was. The city was, and is, full of history and rallies and decision-making. I was hooked. Of course, it also didn't hurt that a week before my birthday, my boyfriend flew out, put a (conflict-free) diamond ring on my finger at the National Botanic gardens, and said that whatever God was going to call me to do, he wanted to be there to see it. As I wrapped up my Washington semester, I was pretty high on life. I was also in awe that the journey that had begun in November 2002 with a Christmas catalog had led me to where I was now shaking hands with Bono and making posters for rallies in front of the White House.

Basically, every day of my college experience was twinged with Zambia. I won't claim that I stopped spending money on myself. But after watching God use Wheaton Academy the way He did and then seeing firsthand the impact on Kakolo village, things that otherwise would have been pretty important to me were suddenly not so important. Now, as a wife and some-day soon, a mother, I try to fill our home with things which remind us that the world is much bigger than Wheaton, Illinois. As an externally-motivated person, the things I look at every day have a profound effect on my mood and my thoughts, so just one memento that reminds me of Zambia or another overseas trip helps me to stay centered and grounded in what I believe God is calling me to do: think globally and to help others do the same. Maps displayed as art are a great way to do this. Wooden bowls bought at the Victoria Falls market in Zimbabwe and pictures of my husband working at a Christian radio station in Guam are constant, tangible reminders for me of our place in God's story of humankind.

One of the biggest repercussions of the Zambia Project in my life has been the challenge of how to apply global thinking to everyday, seemingly mundane choices. I do think that most of the time when my husband and I make a financial decision, Zambia is in the back of our minds, and I hope it stays that way. I went without a car throughout my undergraduate years, which was pretty hard to do in the cornfields of Indiana. Even now, my husband and I have committed to living with only one car. Whenever the weather in the Chicago area allows, my husband bikes to work and I walk.

Finances truly are not an obstacle for God, and I know that I should be willing to step into whatever career He has for me. But at the same time, I now realize that the resources I have are not my own. Looking forward to the future, I know that Zambia has made me, and will continue to make me, more mindful of the power that our economy has over other countries. That applies even to the food we eat and the way we spend our free time. The reality is that the way we choose to spend our money is every bit as powerful as the people we vote into office.

Financial responsibility is something conservatives are always so proud to have down pat: you know, living within one's means and fulfilling existing obligations before taking on new projects. We can even apply the concept of responsibility in personal, everyday spending by researching a grocery store or clothing brand before giving them our hard-earned money. Everyday decisions like where to buy your coffee or your gas have life-shattering repercussions for the people who harvest that coffee or deal with the pollution of an oil spill. It's as if we have the opportunity to be a philanthropist every day. Heiresses and millionaires are practically courted by charities, which need their contributions to exist. Why not force companies to court us with their stellar environmental track records and fair employee treatment?

Theologically, the Zambia Project has created some serious tension for me over the years. At first I wasn't sure how to jive my newfound interest in social justice issues with my previously held beliefs about the gospel and Christian living. In my experience, the people who talked about Christ being the bringer of our salvation were not usually the same people who talked about writing to your congressional representatives, unless the issue was abortion. The people who cared the most about issues like fair trade and clean water were not at all on the same page as the conservative Christians in my hometown. I couldn't, and often still can't, connect the Christ story I see being told in my community with the Christ I see being lived out by people on the opposite end of the political spectrum.

The only answer I have found comes, of course, from Christ Himself. The reality is that Christ showed up on earth in the flesh. We were too stupid to get it any other way. He made it tangible: a Lord in the form of a man who wore sandals and ate tilapia and liked to sleep, but didn't get to very often. Sound familiar? That's what He was supposed to be, familiar and tangible and truly incarnated. So why do we shy away from putting time and money into anything except explicitly laying out the gospel over and over? It's certainly not what Jesus did. Instead, He saved a family from embarrassment at a wedding by providing more wine than they possibly could have needed. He stopped a woman's internal bleeding. He smeared mud on blind eyes, fed people barley loaves and fish, and spared mothers and fathers and sons and daughters from a myriad of life-threatening, life-altering diseases. That was how He piqued people's curiosity. And ironically, meeting their physical needs always made them hungry for more than food and water. He didn't send them away with a tract. He often told people who He was, but most of the time people just knew Him when they saw Him. They knew Him when they saw their leprosy melt away or saw their family member come back from the dead. And you are really going to try to tell me that public health has no place in evangelism?

Which brings me, of course, back full circle to the same dilemma: what role does the political process play? I don't know fully, but I do know that God healed physical ailments then, and he is doing it now all over the world to bring Himself glory. All I know is that I want to be a part of it. In the Christian life responsibility has a much deeper meaning than the surface duties we perform every day in order to assure others that we are trustworthy. Really, I think it means recognizing our place in others' lives and in world history and acting accordingly every day. Basically, it's not about you and I. More than anything else, the Zambia Project has taught me the simple underlying principle that should run beneath everything I choose to pursue: obedience is better than sacrifice. To heed is better than the fat of rams. In other words, recognizing where God is working and then joining Him in that work is always better than conjuring up another great-sounding committee or ministry arm out of my own imagination. That was really why the Zambia Project began in the first place. A crazy bunch of kids barely old enough to drive just sat down and prayed to be used. As it turns out, it's a pretty dangerous prayer, especially when you consider the responsibility that comes with it.

Laura is a graduate of Taylor University and spent four years in state government work before moving to Washington, DC in 2011 to work for Congressman Randy Hultgren (IL-14). Her legislative portfolio includes family and human rights issues

CHAPTER 8

A ZAMBIAN PERSPECTIVE... TAGGED AT HEART

Fordson Kafweku

Standing in the World Vision Chicago metro office in October 2003 with my boss by my side, together we clasped a huge symbolic check of $53,000 from Wheaton Academy. Tony Frank, a development representative for the World Vision United States office, took pictures of the two excited Zambians celebrating the reality that the check we were holding was the birth of a school in Zambia, halfway around the globe. To me it was like any other event; an event of marking history and a chance to collect memoirs of a great trip to this land of abundance. It was my maiden trip to the Unites States, and every moment was an opportunity to catch and stash away memories and experiences. It did not occur to me at all that the "money" I was holding in my hands would signify the beginning of a great journey of impacting lives of countless people in rural Kakolo near the city of Kitwe. It didn't occur to me that this would be a transformation for both the people of Kakolo Village in Zambia and Wheaton Academy in Chicago. It was a connection at heart birthed by a seed sown on that day, and there was to be no turning back! Wheaton Academy had begun a relationship that was to be as strong as the bond between David and Jonathan in the Scriptures; it was a relationship founded on love, compassion, and commitment to shaping people's destiny for the better. The "check" that was in our hands was written in order to build a brand-new schoolhouse! Yes, you heard it—the first school ever in the Kakolo Village.

There is no better word to describe people giving to development work than the word investment. The truth is that as opposed to a donation, an investment almost always brings returns while a donation can mean anything; it is more of a giveaway, and it may or may not be followed by the givers. An investment brings transformation and often can be seen by all. It is interesting that it has taken me more than ten years of my development work to distinguish a donor from an investor in the context of community development! This fresh understanding of who a "donor" really is makes me place Wheaton Academy high school students where they actually belong—as principal investors in human transformational development.

As someone who was born and bred in a third world country like Zambia, I have been "schooled" to believe that donors (now to be called investors) are wealthy people who have spent more than half of their active life making money. They are people who are tired of chasing life and have nowhere to take the money they have accumulated over the years so they choose to "redeem" or attempt to make a good life in their later years of life. I likened them to people who had realized what King Solomon had referred to in Ecclesiastes when he realized that life was all vanity if it did not reflect God's awesome love for us and divine purposes for our lives. Before my encounter with Wheaton Academy high school students, my understanding of these investors was marred. I had a wrong perception! To the contrary, I learned that an investor can be anyone with a vision. These young people were the greatest resource that God raised up as coworkers with Christ to help carve out a path of destiny for many people in Kakolo. They were the anointed of God as they raked in thousands of dollars for their exceedingly beloved Zambian brothers and sisters.

I have always asked myself why these young people chose to help a poverty stricken community of Kakolo when there were millions of such communities all over the world. Why did they keep so close to their dear young hearts a community that was ravaged by HIV and AIDS, and was full of orphans and school dropouts? Why did they embrace children and mothers who were seriously haunted by preventable illnesses, illiteracy, and the non-availability of adequate medical care? Why did they deny themselves the joy of being young Americans who had the privilege of enjoying the wealth of their country, but instead chose to save money to support total strangers with no common identity except being part of God's creation? Why did they come to Africa and visit a continent known for serious diseases such as malaria? The answer lies in God's divine plan and the impact of the Cross. God knew the people of Kakolo from the beginning. He heard their prayers and was set to make a difference through the Wheaton Academy students to the glory and honor of His holy name. Jesus' love for mankind is contagious. When people genuinely avail themselves for service, He does not look at who they are, but what He can do to make them a channel of blessings. He looks at their availability and commitment. He sees only the condition of their hearts and their willingness to serve.

There have truly been several examples of transformational development through the Zamtan Area Development Program. To understand this, a reminder of the community's background is inevitable. Zamtan together with the two neighboring villages of Zambia and Kakolo formed a transit community with makeshift shelters. Truckers employed by the Zambia-Tanzania Road Services would stop over in Zamtan for a day or two while they loaded up and unloaded at the nearby mines. Birthed out of the defunct Road Transport Company which was liquidated in the early 1970s, the people were left in destitution with no social amenities like schools, health facilities, clean and safe water, secure accommodations, and economic development resources. The collapse of the company left many truckers stranded, some of them several kilometers away from their homes of origin. They stayed at this location with no money. The shanty community became their permanent home. With its inhabitants occupying the place with no legal rights and no money, they couldn't afford to improve on their shacks. The people lived in fear of being evicted anytime. The people of this community never had income; most of them contracted themselves for odd jobs to earn a living. Diseases and death especially for children under the age of five and the old were widespread. Offshoots of poverty like alcohol abuse and involvement in anti-social activities were the order of the day. Both the young and the old involved themselves in high-risk activities to earn a living. As the community's population grew, it was evident that the need to provide the community with basic necessities could not be overlooked.

As a result of this need, World Vision, through the permission of local government, obtained authority to start an area development program through which community development interventions would be channeled to develop the community of Zamtan and the surrounding areas. The Zamtan ADP started in 1995 and operated for sixteen years before transitioning in September 2011. The program reached out to a population of about 20,000 Zambians (including over 3,000 sponsored children) for sixteen years. The program implemented interventions including agriculture, health and nutrition, education, water and sanitation, and economic development. Other projects were leadership development, spiritual development, sponsorship, advocacy, and HIV/AIDS. The program's goal was to promote human transformation of the Zamtan community towards improvement in the health, social, economic, spiritual, and community capacity domains until the community was able to manage its own development without requiring further assistance from World Vision.

With a background like this, it's clear that the community was in dire need of external support to facilitate development that would usher in basic services such as health and education. World Vision Zambia's presence for over a decade and a half has significantly transformed the three communities that form the Zamtan Area Development Program. The most evident change has been in the general economic well-being of the people. From a squatter community with shacks as the only form of housing, the economic development projects facilitated by World Vision Zambia have resulted in many affording tin roofed brick houses. After negotiating for Zamtan to be legalized as a permanent settlement, World Vision facilitated the local electricity company to extend hydroelectric power to the community. Another development was the provision of several water wells and other basic needs such as promotion of agriculture and nutrition projects. One major project was the construction of the Zamtan Prevention of Mother to Child Transmission (PMTCT) clinic which brought a much needed medical facility to the community's doorsteps. Other vital facilities such as health posts and Kakolo School were built in Kakolo. Orphans and vulnerable children received new housing units, were given an opportunity to receive an education, and their households were put on microenterprise development activities to sustain their livelihood.

As a result of these projects, the general livelihood of the people in these communities changed for the better. Children enrolled into schools, deaths and sickness were cut significantly, people started utilizing their ideas to access small grants/loans to start small businesses like chicken and pig farming, trading, and general agriculture. The communities that were desolate started booming with several small businesses as people's lives continued to grow. Several of the members in these communities regained their dignity and gradually became self-sufficient as they could now afford to take care of their families and pay the fees needed to send their children to school.

In World Vision programming, sustainability truly is the key underlying principle for all projects. The focus in the final years of a program is to ensure that sustainable processes and institutions are firmly in place in the community. At the household level, from the World Vision perspective, it means that families are able to consistently and fully cater to their needs, and especially the needs of their children. Sustainability means that children are healthy and remain healthy. Schools are educating children. It means that the environment is not sacrificed for the short-term needs of economic development. Prior to leaving, World Vision hands over the community projects to the community including some assets as per policy and decision made by all the stakeholders in the program. When World Vision leaves, it means that their role has ended and the community assumes 100% responsibility. The community and other local partners including the government, the church, and other community-based organizations take over the management of projects for sustainability.

The journey of transformational development is to ensure there is long-term change in the way people live. The success resulting from the existence of World Vision in the community (at least fifteen years) is measured in the exhibition of general improvement in the well-being of the community and the community's capacity to sustain them. Anything short of this will mean the partnership between the community and World Vision has failed to yield the desired result. Being able to attend a beautiful ceremony this past August marking the achievement of self-sustainability as World Vision left the Zamtan area confirmed that God had indeed done a great work in this place. That first check I held in a Chicago office had led to a truly remarkable impact.

Reflecting on the many years of this relationship journey, I see far reaching and inestimable impact. The community of Kakolo will never be the same again. I remember countless times as Program Manager visiting the village of Kakolo, and the mothers would always share how they feared for the lives of their children crossing the busy road to go to the nearest school. Every year, many children lost their lives as they attempted to cross the busy Kitwe Ndola dual carriage way to attempt to receive an education. Certainly, one cannot imagine how many lives have been saved as a result of the Wheaton Academy School in Kakolo! In a country where education is a lifeline, many children that are now schooling at the school in Kakolo will grow to become responsible citizens and role models, and they will certainly contribute to the economy of Zambia as they help their current and future families. On August 13, 2011, I visited Kakolo School and it was amazing to see this vision had unfolded into a huge school with classroom blocks, laboratories, staff houses, clean water, and indeed, hydroelectricity! I was so impressed and felt a sense of satisfaction to see that this school was still growing to accommodate more students and teachers. The community was just as determined as they were in 2003 to see that the school grows into a high functioning high school. This development has transformed a place that was poor, desolate, and forgotten to a beacon of hope and prosperity. God's story is unfolding. The place is slowly becoming a place of choice as it has become the envy of many surrounding villages.

Ryan Souders, one of the first members of the Wheaton Academy team who visited Kakolo in August 2004, left an indelible mark on my heart. During this particular visit, Ryan would from time to time say, "Just do it!" I admit that during that time the statement meant nothing, except that it was being used when having fun as the students interacted with the community, especially during the social and celebratory soccer matches that delighted the children and adults in the community. I remember each time he showed up, children would mob him, shouting, "Do it! Do it! Do it!" The question is: did it really mean anything? Maybe not at that time, but certainly looking back, I realize there was a spiritual force behind it. God had tagged these young people's hearts and continuously encouraged and cheered them to "do it!" Yes, in response to God's call, they called to one another with a compelling voice to serve, saying "Just Do It!" They were surely moved to action!

These young students from Wheaton have always had their own share of extraordinary escapades and experiences in Zambia. Except for a few that returned to Kakolo for a second visit, each year brought in different students with different experiences and expectations. One common experience I saw was that all my visitors could not hold back tears, especially when they saw how, despite their own poverty, the community received them with open hands and friendly hearts. Even in their situation of deprivation, the radiant warmth of these community members could not go unfelt. In my years of working with World Vision, I have often seen visitors deeply moved as they connect with their brothers and sisters in Zambia. Many of them have gone back transformed, not just because of what they have seen, but because God had "visited" them while in Africa, and has given them a different worldview of what each person's life can be. I have seen visitors who have struggled to go back home because they had just fallen head over heels in love with Zambia, and if it were possible they would want to stay on and do everything they could to be a part of God's divine story in these communities. They had seen opportunities to serve in God's massive vineyard of mankind. There is no other reason why Wheaton Academy under the leadership of the Holy Spirit lasted this long in this ministry project. It is not a ministry of feelings; it is a ministry of the heart. It is the project filling that void in one's heart that gives life to a person. Of all the investors from Chicago I have met, I can hardly think of any that have not been touched and transformed in one way or another. God has tagged their hearts for His service to His hurting world when they come to this place called Zambia.

Fordson has a Master in Organizational Leadership from Eastern University, USA, and Bachelor of Science in Tropical Agriculture from Larenstein Professional University in the Netherlands. He also holds a university diploma in Agricultural Engineering from Lusaka, Zambia, and post graduate qualifications in development from the University of South Africa. He worked for the Zambia government as an instructor at Zambia College of Agriculture in Northern Zambia before joining World Vision Zambia in 1998. While with World Vision Zambia, he has served in various positions including working with the organization's Advisory Council as Board Development and Project Manager. He is currently the Director of Operations in charge of World Vision Zambia's field programs.

HOW KAKOLO GOT A NEW SOCCER FIELD

Stephan Leman

I was sitting in the office of my internship the summer between my junior and senior years of college when I received an e-mail from my friend Greg Greg and I were both on Project LEAD together and we had traveled with the team to Kakolo Village just a few years earlier. Any correspondence from Greg this summer was something I looked forward to as he was at the time living in Zambia and working in the community. I enjoyed living vicariously through him sitting in my high-rise office building as he told me tales of the children, his village activities, and how he was introducing them to the game of baseball.

On this particular day, Greg told me about how the Kakolo community wanted to do something in partnership with an anonymous donor to commemorate and thank Chip and Wheaton Academy's devotion to the village over the years. Initially, the item being donated was not defined, but we knew it needed to be something that would stand as a lasting memorial to the work that God had done in that village. We exchanged communications for a bit, but ultimately Greg proposed the idea that represented the best link between Chip, Wheaton Academy, and Zambia: a soccer field.

When Greg and I talked about the notion of building a soccer field in Kakolo Village, it just made sense to us and was an appropriate representation of the original vision of our Project LEAD team. It would be an actual sporting field at the location of the schoolhouse—our "Field of Dreams."

What made the idea of this field even more compelling was the thought of what it would mean for the people of the village as well. After making two trips to Kakolo Village, the most amazing moments of community I think I have ever encountered happened when the whistle blew and the soccer game began. We had the opportunity to take the field and face off against our African brothers as the entire community came out to watch, cheer everyone on, and enjoy the beauty of the game.

After playing there and experiencing the passion for the game in person, it was evident that soccer is a conduit to community in Kakolo, and placing the new soccer field in that village seemed like a natural extension of the work that we had begun years earlier with the schoolhouse. It was an opportunity for people to learn together, to grow together, and hopefully experience fellowship and community around something they loved.

After getting to know Chip over my four years of high school—as a teacher, coach, mentor, and friend—and continuing my friendship with him afterwards, the soccer field in Kakolo Village seems to represent all of his passions. It represents the sport that he loves, the cause and the people that he has embraced, the students that he shares his passion with, and the work of the God that he serves faithfully. My hope is that for years to come children in Kakolo will continue to attend the schoolhouse and rush outside afterwards each day to play soccer on the pitch. Their education quality will never be quite what I was afforded here in the United States, but in some way I hope that the similar experience they are granted will ultimately let them experience God in the same way that I did. The construction of the soccer field in Chip's honor is the perfect culmination to the journey that God took us on over the years in connecting students in Wheaton, Illinois to their brothers and sisters in Kakolo Village, Zambia.

Stephan graduated from Taylor University and works as a research consultant, exploring the motivations and underlying drivers of human behavior for an international brand strategy firm in Chicago, Illinois.

CHAPTER 9

PAIN IN THE PROCESS

If I am to be an honest and transparent narrator of this story, I have to include this chapter on the ups, downs, struggles, and difficulties in the journey of my own life and the lives of hundreds of others over the last nine years. I am often quite averse to conflict due to a personality that loves to build networks of relationships with all kinds of people, and I clearly like to be at peace rather than at odds with the folks around me. And yet my involvement with the issues of AIDS and poverty and justice brought more conflict and discomfort and opposition into my quiet and peaceful little life than I really ever imagined or even perhaps wanted there to be as a Christian educator and leader. Over the course of many years of choosing to focus on responding to the needs of the people in one of the poorest and sickest communities on the planet, several different issues came up that pushed back against our desire to see this movement grow and become all that we believed God wanted it to be. Here are the major stumbling blocks that often felt like potential roadblocks to seeing this project flourish:

Apathy and ignorance toward overwhelming need

For many of the students in our community, poverty and real need simply never has intersected with their daily lives. It is a few miles, a few cities, few states, a few nations, a few continents away from the world where they live, eat, drive, purchase, and sleep. Apathy toward the Zambia Project was a barrier that was often hard to break through as we sought to penetrate the world of programs and stuff that shielded eyes from seeing the need and locked up hearts from being broken by suffering and injustice. The complexity of our world can lead to a sort of paralysis where we choose inactivity and do nothing to change that which we know cannot be right because it just seems like it won't truly accomplish much in the end.

Very real prejudice, stigma, judgment, and perhaps most of all, ignorance were present and were obstacles that caused there to be many moments of tension, challenge, anger, and deep levels of frustration in trying to create a movement to care deeply about the issues facing sub-Saharan Africa. We may have moved forward from the moment when a student asked me if I was scared to hug our family friend and international communicator Princess Kasune Zulu because of her HIV-positive status, but we still found ourselves often dealing with a lack of honest concern about our project. One of the most basic realities for students today in America is the proliferation of activities, devices, entertainment options, and relationship challenges that daily invade their existence. In a strange and warped way, there becomes a parallel in our minds to our need to get the latest Apple product with the need for a child in Africa to receive breakfast before walking several miles to school. And we can unknowingly attempt to pursue a blissful state of detachment where we aren't bothered or troubled as we glide along without wading into the waters of pain and need that prompt us to do something to change the way things are and will be.

The evangelism vs. social justice debate...the fears that we don't care about the gospel and the reality of sin anymore

The occasionally spoken words in public and more regularly believed in private concerning our work in Zambia was that we were justifying the behaviors of those who chose to participate in sexually immoral behaviors. There are obviously consequences for our actions that we cannot avoid if we make certain choices in our lives. However, as we looked at how Jesus Himself interacted with, pursued, and brought healing to the lives of those who were sick, sinful, and broken in His own culture, we could no longer write off helping those who suffered as a result of AIDS as being something we didn't have to do because of the morality of a personal lifestyle choice.

In fact, we saw Jesus go out of His way to debunk the notion that there was a correlation between what one's parents or he or she had done being the justification for a life of blindness they were then made to suffer. Here is a key interaction between Jesus and His own disciples in John 9:1-3, 6-7:

> As he went along, he saw a man blind from birth. His disciples asked him, "Rabbi, who sinned, this man or his parents, that he was born blind?" "Neither this man nor his parents sinned," said Jesus, "but this happened so that the works of God might be displayed in him.... After saying this, he spit on the ground, made some mud with the saliva, and put it on the man's eyes. "Go," he told him, "wash in the Pool of Siloam" (this word means "Sent"). So the man went and washed, and came home seeing.[33]

We have also obviously discovered that the scope of the impact of the disease called AIDS extends so far beyond just the male homosexual community in the Western world and the lives of promiscuous African truck drivers in the global South. We have played with so many HIV-infected children who were given the disease at birth in the most innocent and pure of moments; brought corn meal and cooking oil to young mothers suffering from AIDS who were infected by their husbands who had contracted the disease while out working in another part of the country where work could be found; gotten to know the personal stories of HIV positive women who earn income selling their bodies nightly because it is the only way they can put food into the mouths of the children they love just as much as I love Olivia and Trey; and even had coffee in Wheaton with friends who have lost jobs and apartments because their status was discovered.

The brokenness of our relationships and our world is undeniable in every rural village and every wealthy major metropolitan area. Jesus calls us into the mess and empowers us to be His hand of touch and love, His feet bringing medicines and medical care, and His heart of love that knows no boundaries, no statuses when it comes to seeking to take that which is broken and try to put it back together. None of us deserve the matchless grace and mercy found at the Cross, and yet God gives out this incredible grace and mercy without finding fault to all who would allow it to come into their lives. We all deserve and sometimes do reap the consequences of our sins, but thanks be to Jesus who brings restoration and healing to us even when we haven't done anything to warrant that most extraordinary response.

Another of the strongest and most persistent criticisms from my fellow Christians has been the notion that we are doing social justice work only and neglecting the greater mandate to share verbally the good news of Jesus with people who do not identify themselves as Christians. I've been told that our work is no different than the good things being done to try to help people and save lives in Africa by people like Oprah and Brad Pitt and Madonna. We've been accused of sending people to hell who are more educated, healthier, and well fed when they leave this earth and face eternity. To be honest, this debate is one that at times has caused me to both consider stopping our work in Africa and consider leaving formal Christian education and ministry in the evangelical setting. In the midst of this very real tension and confusion as I listened to the lessons of my upbring-ing and education, the words of many of my respected friends, and the voices of the children of Africa all speaking into my ears, I have found myself turning my eyes back to a passage that I can never get away from as I consider what Jesus would have me do with my life in Matthew 25:34-40:

> *The King will say to those on his right, "Come, you who are blessed by my Father, inherit the Kingdom prepared for you from the creation of the world. For I was hungry, and you fed me. I was thirsty, and you gave me a drink. I was a stranger, and you invited me into your home. I was naked, and you gave me clothing. I was sick, and you cared for me. I was in prison, and you visited me." Then these righteous ones will reply, "Lord, when did we ever see you hungry and feed you? Or thirsty and give you something to drink? Or a stranger and show you hospitality? Or naked and give you clothing? When did we ever see you sick or in prison and visit you?" And the King will say, "I tell you the truth, when you did it to one of the least of these my brothers and sisters, you were doing it to me!"[34]*

Somewhere along my many readings of this passage and my listening to a podcast from pastor and speaker Francis Chan I began to wrestle deeply with these questions that still flare up in my mind so often: *What if Jesus really meant what He said? What if Jesus really is concerned about how I treat the least at the level of judgment and priority He expresses in Matthew's Gospel?*

And out of this look at Jesus' words here and years of experiences and engagement with the ideas concerning evangelism, the gospel, and justice so present in the whole of Scripture I have arrived at a few guiding thoughts that give me clarity in the debate:

I believe that the best response to Scripture is to see what God has called us to do in relationship to "social justice" work and evangelism as being designed to be partners rather than stand-alone activities. The task of making the gospel known involves both proclamation and demonstration as we offer the hope of Christ for this life and the life to come. The combination of both word and deed is the most powerful apologetic for this faith called Christianity in a world filled with good ideas, incredible needs, and broken lives.

The reality is that the meeting of physical need is often what needs to be done in order for spiritual engagement and healing to take place. To be perfectly honest, if we don't help provide ARV's (anti-retro viral medicines) for people suffering from AIDS and help reduce their CD4 counts and help their body to fight against this deadly infection in sub-Saharan Africa, many of them will die and be faced with the question of their eternal destiny before we can talk with them about this Jesus who has died so that they may live. Physical healing was so often done by Jesus in connection with spiritual life change, and those stories are so clear that I can't help seeking to follow that model myself.

Despite some of the words you have read above that could cause you to at least wonder if I have lost my interest in the state of people's souls, there is nothing I want my life to be about more than introducing people to Jesus Christ. There is absolutely no doubt that the thing that people need and are designed to do is to be in relationship with the One who offers healing for the sickness that sin creates in our relationship with God, other people, and the world. I am more and more convinced that the broken world I have seen more up close than ever before needs the mending of heart, body, and soul that is found only at the Cross.

For much of my life I have had a desire and felt the pressure to tell non-Christ followers about who Jesus is and the opportunity they have to experience salvation and forgiveness through a personal relationship with Him. However, because of my professional position in ministry and Christian education settings, this evangelistic work has been somewhat of a personal struggle to do because of the Christian environment I spend much of my time in and the reputation that comes along with being a "campus or church pastor" or "Bible teacher." I would often try to break through that bubble by participating in avenues in our culture such as athletics as a soccer coach or neighborhood activities as a homeowner. I enjoyed those relationships and occasionally would get to the place where I would invite someone I had gotten to know to a church service or a Bible study, and often tried to use the questions about what I did for a living even by those I would randomly meet as transitions to share with them the story of who Christ was and what He had done on their behalf. I often felt guilty about not doing more evangelism as a spiritual leader of others and was frustrated with the seeming indifference to the biblical ideas presented even when I did get the chance to provide a verbal witness about my faith journey and the gospel itself.

Surprisingly, the greatest time of evangelistic opportunity and engagement with people who do not know Jesus and have not experienced His remarkable grace and redemption in their lives has come during the course of my working on the Zambia Project. As evidenced by the incredible cultural interest and acceptance of programs like the ONE Campaign, American Idol Gives Back, Save Darfur Coalition, and the Haiti Earthquake response, people are drawn to movements and people who are creating opportunities to help those attempting to deal with the greatest of needs in our world today. My own involvement in the global AIDS pandemic and the cycle of poverty in Zambia has spurred on more meaningful conversations about my faith and the Jesus in whose name I am doing all of these things, than in perhaps all the other thirty years of my life before I was involved in serving and caring for the poor in a meaningful way.

Soccer coaches who were across the field from me for many years gathered equipment from their players for us to take to African soccer players and read my blogs about our trips in Zambia. I have sent pieces of the rough draft of this text to a sportswriter friend for him to read while he was sitting poolside in Las Vegas. Public school administrators, teachers, and students wanted to hear our story to the point of allowing us to come on their campus to share our project, and even joined us on our overtly Christian trip to Zambia as partners in creating unprecedented opportunities for education for children in north central Zambia. Many of them have become lifelong friends.

And almost everywhere I have traveled all over our country and even in my own backyard, I find myself talking about the purpose I've found in being the hands and feet of Jesus among the poorest of the poor to the greatest variety of people I've ever known in my life. Doing the work of social justice has given me a platform and point of spiritual engagement to talk about Jesus on a level that finally gets closer to the vision I've had for so long about introducing people to Jesus in a relational and compelling manner. These opportunities to share the gospel story came not because of my brilliant arguments for the validity of the message or the entertainment value of a fantastic church event; they emerged and were extended by nonbelievers because they saw that my life and the lives of my students were being spent on seeking to serve and meet the needs of others. This commitment to service and the attempt at living a missional lifestyle caused them to be willing to hear about the One who mandated and modeled it best in the pages of the Gospels.

Fatigue of sticking with a project long enough to achieve real community change

A few years ago I remember talking to a key staff person at World Vision who expressed that the thing he was most surprised about concerning our Zambia Project was simply the length of its run in a center place in our community. He said we were way past the curve where a global initiative typically maintains life and energy before dying off. In almost all of my ministry experiences over the last twenty years, the initiatives tended to be ones that we would create, present, drive really hard for a few months, and then celebrate before meeting again to determine what the next thing needed to be to grab the attention of our people once again. In a culture that has even speeded up significantly in terms of distractions and options and information over the life of our work in Zambia, it has been a miracle of sorts that we did the same school year project for nine straight years.

In almost every year of the Zambia Project, there would be a conversation that highlighted the comments student leaders would hear from some of their peers and even their own questions about rolling out the same type of thing year after year: "Haven't we done enough for the people of this one community? We have clearly done more than they could have ever expected from a group of kids in America!" "Why should we limit our impact to just one place when there are so many needs in every community across the world?" "People are getting sick and tired of hearing about poverty and AIDS in chapels every week." "Isn't it really impossible to think that we can help alleviate poverty and disease in a place where it is so bad right now?" "The Zambia buzz was great, but now it is gone."

These questions really did threaten to end a project before I thought it was time to do so, and in many ways it was often a pretty courageous decision by a determined group of students to continue to push this initiative forward with conviction and creativity and a sense of deep calling when the words they heard all around them didn't always support or endorse the vision they were trying to cast in the name of Jesus. But in the end, hanging in there and working for several years on projects serving the same community was surprisingly and arguably the best decision we could have ever made. I think God would have been OK with just one year of response from our community, but ultimately God simply wouldn't let us drop it. We never received permission from Him to let go of that which He called us to do.

And perhaps most significantly, the greatest benefit is simply the building of a real friendship. The reality is, by continuing to invest our financial resources, our prayers, our time, and our love, authentic and cross-cultural friendships that mean a lot to people on both sides of the ocean have been formed.

The Zambia "Project" has truly turned into the Zambia "Partnership." We have scores of Facebook friends and posts connecting people an eighteen-hour plane ride apart from one another. We talk about the Kakolo community to others using "our village" language. Pictures of Zambians still hang in American offices from five years ago while photos of "muzungus" from America are in the cubicles of World Vision Zambia offices in a Zambian neighborhood. We have visited and truly feel at home at each other's residences. And we look forward expectantly to that day when we will no longer just be able to see one another once a year at best, but rather spend eternity together in God's village where we will live in perfect community celebrating how God has brought us together in such unexpected ways.

Giving to others overseas will take away from our own fundraising, ministry needs, and projects at home

I still remember some very early honest conversations with our former headmaster about whether or not it made sense for Wheaton Academy to be involved in simultaneous fundraising endeavors for our community's needs and expansion in West Chicago, Illinois, along with a major initiative on behalf of a community in Zambia. Our dialogue led us eventually to a shared belief that God wanted us to seek to do both rather than choosing one or the other. In fact, I am truly amazed that the school allowed us incredible freedom to raise rather large amounts of resources for people in Africa while being in the midst of needing millions of dollars to fund their own building projects and scholarship needs as our student body continued to grow.

However, I also have at times felt incredible tension between the needs of people in absolute poverty in Zambia and the desires to keep a Christian high school functioning at an excellent level in suburban American culture. I know that members of both our board and administrative team at selected points have often viewed this project with questions and concerns. In many cases where I have tried to inspire other Christian schools to start their own "Zambia Project" they have immediately told me that there is no way that their schools could ever raise money for people in Africa when they have such significant pressures to raise money for their own schools every day. And I have felt almost daily the struggle to care about what is going on elsewhere when the challenges of my own family, job, and ministry seem very large without inviting the massive needs of another group of people into my life circle.

I think that the group that has struggled most concerning these seeming competing interests are the students who have led this project and seen firsthand the needs of people in Zambia on our vision trips. At our debrief times after being with children and seeing the living conditions and realities faced by families in African communities, they would finally let go and voice the questions that burned so deep in their young and idealistic minds:

"How can we possibly be spending lots of money on a new gym at our school when there are over seven hundred kids squashed into a two-room schoolhouse where they are being educated for the first time in their community history?"

"How can our church be raising millions of dollars for a new building when the church I am in on Sunday in Zambia has holes I can see the sky through in the thatch roof that covers their humble brick wall structure?"

I would often sit speechless and shrug my shoulders in these group conversations, which to be honest, is a rarity for an extroverted teacher such as myself. I have and continue to battle the very same questions and emotions that they do; I just think I am better sometimes at compartmentalizing them or explaining them away with complicated rhetoric. But I cannot ultimately escape these questions and they are the tensions that I don't really want my former students and myself to ever choose to put aside because it is just too difficult to deal with them. I've decided most days that I must be a "and" person whom God has called to be a bridge between the vision for growth and impact in Chicago or Grand Rapids and the call of critical physical and spiritual needs so daily present in places far away from our everyday eyes. It's not really about Africa; it's about allowing ourselves to pursue the calling of God on our lives to love our neighbors. It's about becoming people whose lives are others-centered, whether they are across the street or the Atlantic Ocean. I have gone back to a rather simple biblical phrase from Philippians 4:19 where Paul reminds us that,

"My God will meet all your needs according to the riches of his glory in Christ Jesus."[35]

I am left with the conclusion that simply I must trust and believe that God will care for me, care for my family, and care for the needs of our school in divine ways if we step out and give extravagantly to meeting the needs of the poor. I cannot escape the faces of children in Zambia, the incredible dreams of high school students, and the words of Jesus when He draws it down to a clear focus when He told both wealthy and poor people on a mountainside listening to Him over two thousand years ago in Matthew 6:21: "Where your treasure is, there your heart will be also."[36] He knew that the clearest measure of what I most deeply care about is what I spend my money on, and that connection will never change for people all over the world. I can only hope that the things that God cares most about will remain fresh and poignant so I can continue to act rather than be paralyzed by the tensions of convergence of the worlds I live in and have traveled to see.

Questions of whether or not we could really connect deeply with people who live so far away and whose lives look so different than ours

There are startling and obvious cultural differences between Chicago and Zambia, and you often find yourself wondering if you can ever really find enough common ground to truly become friends. It doesn't happen overnight, and it takes each side making a decision to discover what is important and loved in their community and lives. You walk away from conversations and experiences wondering if you really understand what the other person thinks about you, and it is challenging to develop relationships of trust and openness. There are barriers of language, food, resources, and even appearances that can build walls between people who hope to get to know one another. But I have discovered that God can connect a person to someone on the other side of the world through rather unexpected things.

In the summer of 2004 on my first visit to Zambia I took a walk with my friend Fordson who became the kind of friend who would drive from anywhere in the whole nation to share a meal with me when he found out I was coming back to his country. On our walk we dreamed together about what God might want to do in Kakolo Village. He had dreams that were way bigger than I could imagine, dreams that truly were God-sized in the midst of completely overwhelming and devastating poverty. We both pointed to an overgrown field of wild grass and imagined things like electricity, a huge schoolhouse addition, a new medical clinic, clean water wells, a ministry center. And God has seen fit to allow us to help make those dreams become reality. The last thing Fordson talked about was something rather unusual. He turned to an overgrown field spot a couple of hundred yards away with trees and said, "That's where the brand-new soccer pitch must go and you will come back and play on it with us someday."

In 2007, I made a very difficult decision and stepped down as the varsity boys' soccer coach at Wheaton Academy. To be honest, I was left wondering if I had made the right decision or if I was really valued as a coach when I made this decision to quit. I loved coaching, loved my players, and was quite sure I had not truly fulfilled the competitive goals I set out to achieve on the field. As the summer began and the season drew near, I was missing it and feeling very weird about not being a part of a program I had poured my life into. And then we went back to Zambia for our third trip.

I have loved soccer for most of my life, and the people of Zambia play the game every day even without grass, round balls, and nets on goals. It is easy to feel out of place when you first encounter the least, but for me and many of my friends, a soccer ball and a dirt field made us feel very much at home. As we reconnected with our brothers and sisters in Kakolo Village that summer, there was one beautiful brand-new thing the community had built without resources from Wheaton Academy students. By hand over the course of many months, the Kakolo community had built a gorgeous new soccer pitch, with a level dirt playing field, white pipe goals with nets, and skybox seats built on the top of two gigantic anthills overlooking the pitch. It was truly the most beautiful field I had seen in all of our travels throughout the nation, and it was a gift for us, a place where we could play the game together on a field built with love for people who played on perfect grass on the other side of the world.

On the side of the field was a rather large marker that had my name on it as the person whom this field was dedicated to as we played the first match on the field. It was a complete surprise and arguably the best gift I have ever received in my entire life. It was the completion of my dream, Fordson's dream, and God's dream for this community and our relationship as two communities were brought together. As I stepped onto that field to play, I felt remarkably loved and affirmed; and much of the pain in leaving coaching melted away because of the reality that I would always have my field to play and coach on in the years to come. My friends on the other side of the world knew exactly what I loved and whom I loved; and if you ask me what some of the best moments and days in my life have been and will continue to be, I would tell you about playing soccer with those who were once complete strangers. For on the soccer pitch that people in Chicago will never ever see, I am at my second home, playing the game I love with people who have shown me the love of Jesus in a most personal and tangible and sacrificial way. My life is obviously different in its richness and meaning, because of the friendship of the people of Zambia, those that Jesus called the least.

Enduring the actual pain, stress, and grief involved in entering into the deep needs of those who are suffering

I had seen lots of statistics on the poverty and disease present in the world before, but for some reason when I first read quotes from Bono about AIDS and saw the data about life in Zambia, I found them sticking deep in my memory like the performance statistics of my favorite athletes growing up. And when I went once and then twice and then a few more times to African villages and walked in huts where my sponsored children lived and where people literally days if not hours from dying were lying on bamboo mats on the ground beside where I was sitting, I found myself not being able to fit in at home or work when I returned. I just wasn't able to so quickly and easily get right back into that ever familiar and oh so comfortable lifestyle I secretly treasured and sought to manage for the first thirty some years of my life.

I began to sense a new daily stress and challenge in trying to live with the perspective of life where pain and suffering were front and center while continually feeling the push to perform at a high level of creativity and competency in a place where we worked really hard to stay cutting edge in educating and transforming the lives of over six hundred high school students every day. Some days I just wanted to scream out loud and tell everyone to stop for a moment and realize that what we are so worried about in our lives isn't truly reality; reality is looking for food and water and medicine instead of what we spend our time caring about. There was and remains a knowledge that what I do here can hopefully impact and bring change to their lives there, but that understanding of what the world looks like there can often be sobering and leaves a bundle of guilt producing questions about why I am here and my friends are experiencing such a different life there.

I often found myself talking about people and places and needs that others couldn't relate to and had never seen like I had, and frankly, I think people have and continue to get sick of my perspective and communication about the intersection of our lives and the global world. I've ruffled the feathers of those in authority above me despite a rather compliant and easygoing personality, and I've found myself out of place in team settings for the first time in my life. I've somehow become some sort of AIDS and poverty activist/advocate whose ideas don't always jive with the vision of those around me. I can easily feel like a crazy person who is all of a sudden a round peg in the square holes of the evangelical and American board where we seek to drop ourselves into places and positions of security and acceptance. And for a guy who's always been well liked, easily accepted, and firmly planted in the middle of the core of such groups, it is unsettling and unfamiliar to be at the extremes and edges of a community of people.

More than perhaps anything else on a personal level, my involvement with the Zambia Project has done a surgery of sorts on my heart. The combination of getting to know people who are being devastated by diseases like AIDS and malaria and tuberculosis and the incredible examples of family members and caregivers compassionately wrapping their arms around them when they are often sick and poor themselves has done something to move me to places of real concern for those suffering, perhaps to be honest for the first time in my life. I have always been fascinated by how the Son of God was such a feeling and compassionate man in the midst of being the Creator and Ruler of the Universe. I finally saw what that looked like in the way that Zambian Christians lived in the midst of the greatest humanitarian crisis of this generation.

On the surface level, I have often wondered ultimately what this engagement with the suffering of others has been doing to my own soul and spirit and emotional state. A couple of summers ago, I began to see firsthand the good and the bad and the change that has come to my heart, mind, and spirit. The sudden death of a couple of people closely connected to me and repeated scenes of loss seen in Africa sent me into what I have described in my own writings as a sort of "dark night for my soul." I watched the tremendous pain their family members were going through both in Africa and in Chicago, and I found myself worrying everyday what would happen to my family if I left them. I was broken, confused, and in need of some comfort and help and grace.

I've discovered a few years now removed from those events and after another trip to Zambia that I'm still hurting on some level. My life is not idealistic and fancy-free as a guy living the American dream. I still am afraid now and then for some reason that I might die earlier than I want to as a relatively young husband and father. I still shed tears more easily and at inopportune moments when seeing things that are painful and seemingly so unfair. I've learned that there is a danger in entering deeply into the issues and pain of those you know and care about. And I am sure that sharing in the suffering of other people is exactly what God designed us to do in following our compassionate Savior who was regularly broken and distraught at what He saw happening to people in the days He spent living on earth.

If I sat down with you for a couple of hours over a cup of coffee and we talked frankly about the last decade of my life, I would tell you about the curse and the joy of being a part of God's work in sub-Saharan Africa. Several years ago my close friend from World Vision Chicago's office sent me an e-mail sarcastically warning me that someday this AIDS deal might cost me an awful lot if I wasn't careful. I've gotten several e-mails and text messages from some of my closest former students who were deeply involved in this project thanking me for wrecking their life as they consider careers and relationships and their place in this world. They were kidding me and they were not kidding themselves. Sometimes I know they wish they'd never gotten to see what they've seen so they could live without that knowledge and conviction informing their pursuits and faith in this life. I personally can't understand why I am so compelled to care so deeply about this place and people I've only spent about fifty days with in my life. Why do I check the BBC Africa and Zambia Post websites daily on my phone, cheer for the Zambia national soccer team like I do my hometown baseball team, keep planning the next trip to Africa before I get home from the last one, and talk and write about issues affecting Africa just about every day of my life?

The reality of the Zambia Project for me, for hundreds of students, and for our brothers and sisters in Zambia is this: life is not simple, life is often filled with things we wish we could avoid, and life is doable and good and worthwhile. This is because we have a Savior who has entered into our pain and gives us the strength and courage to live with joy and purpose. We can do this in the midst of AIDS and fears and poverty and materialism because of the new life He has given to each of us as we discover it at the Cross. I shared these words from John Stott at a family friend's funeral and they remind me even today of the reality that Jesus has directed me into this work, sustained me through the conflict and challenges it has brought, and longs for all of us to care for the least because He identified most with those who suffered while here on earth as God in the flesh.

I could never myself believe in God if it were not for the cross. In the world of pain, how could one worship a God who was immune to it? In my imagination I have turned over and over to that lonely, twisted, tortured figure on the cross, nails through hands and feet, back lacerated, limbs wrenched, brow bleeding from thorn-pricks, mouth dry and intolerably thirsty, plunged in God-forsaken darkness. That is the God for me! He laid aside His immunity to pain. He entered our world of flesh and blood, tears and death. He suffered for us. Our sufferings become more manageable in light of His. There is still a question mark against human suffering, but over it we boldly stamp another mark—the cross, which symbolizes Divine suffering. The cross of Christ is God's and our only self-justification in such a world as ours.[37]

This particular friend's son Matt, who has been a leader in our Zambia Project and has the "Africa bug" after going on two trips there, talked about what his dad would say to those attending his funeral. His remarkable words as a son grieving offer the reminder as to why it is worth all I have written about and more to be a Matthew

25 disciple of our Lord. He said, "My dad's death was shocking, unexplainable, and we could do nothing about it. But in Africa today over ten thousand people will die from diseases that are eminently treatable. There is no reason for them to die. We can do something to save them, and that's what my dad as a Christian and a doctor would want you to know and to do if he were still here today." I began to weep in my seat and figured after his words I could dismiss people without preaching my message. And hundreds and hundreds of children in Kakolo Village attend school now because of the classroom additions made possible from the funds gathered in Jim Taylor's memory.

I remember thinking that I had never heard those kinds of ideas at a funeral and how surprising it was to hear a recently graduated high school kid offer truly unexpected words at a moment of deep personal pain. Matt was able to see and embrace hope even in the darkest of moments for him personally through the lens of the incarnation. He could do this because He knew this Jesus who had flipped the paradigm for his dad, for him, for me, and for all who follow Him because of what He said and how He lived in the midst of persecution, opposition, and crucifixion. Even as we see the fallen world all around us, we can and must embrace the burden with the help of a Savior who promises to help carry the load. May His radically countercultural words in the Sermon on the Mount continue to invite and inspire us to enter into suffering, be the voice for those who have no voice, and do whatever it takes to be like Him in how we live this different life that will be blessed by Him.

Blessed are the poor in spirit, for theirs is the kingdom of heaven.

Blessed are those who mourn, for they will be comforted.

Blessed are the meek, for they will inherit the earth.

Blessed are those who hunger and thirst for righteousness, for they will be filled.

Blessed are the merciful, for they will be shown mercy.

Blessed are the pure in heart, for they will see God.

Blessed are the peacemakers, for they will be called children of God.

Blessed are those who are persecuted because of righteousness, for theirs is the kingdom of heaven. (Matthew 5:3-10)[38]

LEAVING A LEGACY

Jeff Brooke

"We want Chip. We want Chip. We want Chip." Everyone on the bus turned and stared at me as the sound grew louder as we approached the village of Kakolo. The primary thing that I knew was that I was not Chip, and he wasn't showing up any time soon. The bus we rode into their village was being chased by children, waved at by adults, and cheered for by all. The school name of Wheaton Academy brought a smile to the face of the Zambian people that had reflected a joy that ran deeper than just a quick grin. The community had been changed by the dream of some students who said that God is big, and He has given us a vision that could only come from Him. As I stepped off the bus, I began to see how that vision was not simply written on a white board, talked about in a meeting, or spoken of as simply a school lesson plan. The vision had been real, it ran deep, and it had been pursued like very few I had ever seen. The vision was soaked in prayer, led by God, and had been activated in the lives of the people in Kakolo Village.

The people of Kakolo scanned our faces in search of their celebrity star. As their gazes fell towards me there was confusion. I could clearly see the questions in their minds, "Who are you and why are you here?" Each person was seemingly waiting for a hug, a cheer, a smile, and a cry to honor the God who had brought them together for eternity. I introduced myself as Chip's friend and as only Zambian people can do, they welcomed me and cheered despite their disappointment in not seeing their American friend.

It had been seven years since Chip had missed a yearly trip to the village of Kakolo in northern Zambia. He had asked me to lead the trip instead of him, and little did I know, it would change my heart forever. You see, Chip and

I go way back. He has been my coach, teacher, role model, mentor, leadership trainer, marriage counselor, boss, and friend for the last dozen years. He has been a person in my life who changed the way I thought, the faith I embraced, and the things I chose to pursue. I had never had much interest in global justice, high school students, or education. Yet there I stood, in the dusty streets of Kakolo Village, with ten amazing high school students, a remarkable African school cheering us, and hearts that were seemingly changing by the second.

I played on Chip's soccer field, walked the dusty paths to HIV positive mothers, distributed bikes, delivered small grocery items to broken homes, and cried at the sight of poverty. But it was in a small hut, holding the hand of an AIDS patient that I realized I had been led to a place I would have never gone on my own. I realized the potent combination of leadership passions mixed with the powerful belief in Jesus Christ. I noticed how my life had gone down a different road where I acquired a different heartbeat and a changed mind. God had used a mentor to teach me some new things about the heart of my Savior and the essence of the gospel I proclaim. It was as I said amen and squeezed that lady's hand that God's Spirit nudged me. God has only nudged me a few times, but they are actually more like strong pushes than gentle nudges. They are life altering.

The nudge was a push in the direction of student ministry and social justice. I came to the realization that Chip had led me because God had gripped him and told him to lead students. Chip believed that students are some of the most gifted people on the planet, and I now believe the same. Chip believed that one cannot have full joy unless he is meeting the needs of those who are less fortunate. I have begun to feel that same hunger for justice in our world. He believes that the greatest test of a leader actually comes in the wake of his absence. I have been stung with a burning desire to empower students, teach the need for justice, and empower others to lead in ways that are better than my own.

Now, as I serve in some of the same roles Chip once held, I begin to think of what has yet to happen. My mind quickly drifts to what God might continue to do with His high school students. This year at Wheaton Academy we launched a new project that will seek to do similar things that the Zambia Project once did. God has moved us to support a thriving church in Port-au-Prince, Haiti. The students of Wheaton Academy have researched, traveled, prayed, and listened for the past year. We are thrilled to move forward with a project that will provide immediate support for twenty different orphans and hopefully indirectly shape a community.

The beauty of leadership seems to be seen years after the primary leader has moved on. I believe Chip will walk the campus of Wheaton Academy many years down the road and see many reminders of his time there. He will see the orange bricks with Zambian names on them, he will see photographs of Zambian people he fell in love with in the Fine Arts Center, and he will find old T-shirts which say, "Dodgeball for Zambia." But, I am quite sure he will not be satisfied by those types of memories. He will only be satisfied when he sees that the pursuit of the gospel, the pursuit of global justice, still continues at a school of six hundred that is seeking to teach students that Jesus is a God of love, a God of relationship, and a God of grace.

Then, in that moment, Chip will realize what God wanted to do with him at Wheaton Academy. In that moment, he will know this was not just about Zambia; it was about implanting a passion into the DNA of a school. It was about us becoming a school that will always seek to teach students how to care for people as Jesus so graciously cared for us. And maybe someday, he and I will play soccer with the next leader on that Zambian dirt soccer field.

Jeff has a master's degree from Crown College (MN) and has served as the Director of Victory Sports Camps. He is currently a Bible Teacher, the Director of Student Leadership and Service, and the Varsity Boys Soccer Coach at Wheaton Academy.

CHAPTER 10

THE NEXT CHAPTER FOR STUDENTS AT WHEATON ACADEMY, CORNERSTONE UNIVERSITY, KAKOLO VILLAGE SCHOOLHOUSE, AND YOU AND I

One of the most fascinating parts of this story is that this relationship between Wheaton and Zambia now runs so deep that it has become pretty much impossible to end. As our long-term project in Kakolo Village wound down and the community moved closer to self-sustainability, (always the goal of the community development model—hooray!) the next group of students began to explore other opportunities to partner with Kingdom ventures and projects in sub-Saharan Africa. We raised resources to fund some large group loans in microfinance projects in Kenya with a wonderful partner in Opportunity International; and we provided bicycles for children who needed them to be able to get to school each day in another rural village in Zambia through a partnership with the dynamic World Bicycle Relief group. We didn't raise nearly as much money or host as many events on campus, but we still were part of God's Kingdom plan to look outside of ourselves and meet the needs of the least in our world.

I left Wheaton Academy a few years ago to take a new job, wondering what the future would hold for me and for the school in regards to both of our future involvements with issues of global need and Kingdom justice. I've left the high school environment, but student passion for God's global work on that particular campus remains strong through new partnerships with two more communities in Zambia and Haiti. There is great joy for me in watching this take place, and I'm left with a gulp of clear understanding that it is, and has always been, about God and His people, not the leader guy whom people often saw as the front person for the project.

Personally, I still wondered if my new academic community would be interested in places like sub-Saharan Africa and in issues like HIV and clean water. The Christian college I went to work at had roots in a faith system that had definitely emphasized the verbal proclamation of the gospel as the centerpiece of any missions or global involvement work. When I got there, I quickly helped to start a student organization called ACT:S that was part of a World Vision sponsored network of hundreds of university groups that cared about issues of poverty and justice. There was some strong initial interest, but as the school year ended, only a handful of students were coming to our biweekly meetings. I even proposed a trip to Zambia as part of our global opportunities initiatives that I had to cancel due to lack of student interest. The invitations to get involved and help start a new movement on our campus were often received openly by student leaders I talked to, but I didn't see many of them follow through and meet my hopes and expectations with specific actions and initiatives.

I often felt discouraged and wondered whether I should stop trying to engage our student community about the needs of our brothers and sisters around the globe as many in our own student population were dealing with the economic realities of living in Michigan, a state probably affected more by the economic meltdown than any other in our country.

As I seriously thought about stepping back and away from my role as an instigator of student responses to global crisis and needs, I discovered anew that this work God had invited me to experience was now a centerpiece of how Christianity gained expression in my own spiritual journey. And I just couldn't escape the voices in my head and in my heart. They are the voices, the words, the pleas of the children of Zambia and my former high school students who would both beg you and I to do something in response to the story you have read in the previous pages. Here is my retelling of what I have heard them say in the midst of this broken and magnificent world God has created:

The voices of the children of Zambia:

We love wearing our school uniforms and orange backpacks you brought us as we walk to school each day.

We love doing math in a classroom, pumping water at the well, calling for the ball on the soccer pitch, and singing in the front of our thatch-roof church.

We can now sing songs and recite poems and perform skits about the dangers of AIDS because we now understand that it can destroy our lives and our community.

We want to be doctors and nurses so we can help all the people in our families who are sick to get better.

We can't wait to walk with you from our school to our soccer field holding your hand as we get to know all kinds of stuff about one another's lives.

We can see something beyond where we are now, and we long to first of all live, and then to live the life we feel called to pursue.

We want you to know that Africa is not what you have seen or what you think. It is full of courageous and talented and ambitious young people—many who love God deeply and have been praying with great faith that they will be the ones to change their villages, their countries, and their continent as they become new leaders who live with integrity, joy, vision, and grace.

We need you to believe that if you do something, you will change a life, and when you change a life, perhaps my life, you will never, ever regret what you have done.

While in Zambia, I have this immense pleasure of watching a group of normal seventeen to twenty-two-year olds do something remarkable. They actually fall in love with a people and a culture that offers them very little of what they have been trained to believe they need to be happy. Every week I have spent in Zambia I have seen teenagers hold and carry children who look and often are quite ill without being concerned about the spread of germs. They have played games like Red Rover and Duck, Duck Goose and run around for hours in the African dirt. They've chosen to sleep with mosquito nets over their beds and to make getting stranded in the Zambian night due to bus problems a great adventure. And most of all, they've discovered and then affirmed to one another that getting outside of oneself and entering into another's suffering is perhaps what we were most designed to do.

I've included so many pieces of student writing in this book because they are the ones who have discovered and displayed what it means to follow in the example of a Savior who loved and touched and valued the sick and poor and oppressed and different in a day and time when you weren't supposed to do that as a person of religious convictions. I've savored so many nighttime group conversations with my students after spending the day with the people of Zambia over the last several years. The passion and the love and the belief in and for the work of justice and restoration are so palpable and almost shocking when you hear it firsthand. Here's my summary of the words I've heard this generation speak in these huddles to the church and the world in this day and age:

The voices of the students in this generation:

Don't keep giving us stuff with the thought that it will fulfill us and make us happy. The more we get, the harder it is to know what we should value most in this life.

The lives of the children all over the globe matter just as much as our own. Just because we were born in a different location simply does not give us the right to have a chance to pursue our dreams while others do not.

The irony is that when we are in other places and with people from other cultures, we actually find things more engaging and exciting than our own world that we've always been told is simply the best.

We believe that the heart of God expressed in Scripture is to be an advocate for justice and compassion and mercy in a world where competition and self-reliance wants to rule the day.

Students have access to the kind of financial and relational resources that can truly change communities and lives if they make the decision to release their creativity and push back against the materialism of the American culture.

We do want to be a generation that makes the world a place less affected by poverty, disease, racism/culturalism, and oppression.

It is time for the church here to stop being arrogant and to learn and copy the practices of other global faith communities.

If you step out in faith and take some risks in dreaming and then following through with taking on the biggest problems and issues in our world today, God will show up and multiply the bread and fish you gather to feed and heal more than you can ever believe.

The voices of the children of Zambia and the young people of this generation are remarkably strong, and their words are clearly pointed in seeking a response in the lives of those of us who name Jesus as Lord. But more than the words of African children who immediately grab hearts and the teenagers who are often maligned and discarded, there is a voice that is the ultimate voice, the voice of the inspired words of Scripture that I invite you to read again below as this book's final chapter is written:

**Here is the voice of the One who has created, redeemed, and
is in the process of restoring all lives and things even today:**

> *No, this is the kind of fasting I want:*
> *Free those who are wrongly imprisoned;*
>   *lighten the burden of those who work for you.*
> *Let the oppressed go free,*
>   *and remove the chains that bind people.*
> *Share your food with the hungry,*
>   *and give shelter to the homeless.*
> *Give clothes to those who need them,*
>   *and do not hide from relatives who need your help....*
> *Feed the hungry,*
>   *and help those in trouble.*
> *Then your light will shine out from the darkness,*
>   *and the darkness around you will be as bright as noon.*
> *(Isaiah 58:6-7, 10)*[39]

I've discovered that the voices of my friends in Chicago and
Zambia followed me to Grand Rapids, and keep whispering in my
ear wherever I go. I am quite sure I will never be able to go somewhere
that they cannot be heard.

One of the loudest and most familiar voices in my life has always
been the voice of those who are athletes. College athletes on most
campuses across our country are often the superstars of the community, attracting admiration and adulation by the large group gatherings that watch them perform. Strangely enough, this isn't always the
case on our campus. The men's soccer team has had a negative reputation for some questionable lifestyle choices and seeming arrogance
toward other student groups. The men's basketball team that won a
national championship often plays home games with little more than
a handful of current students in the stands. In a somewhat bizarre

way, some of our student athletes were "the least" in the way they were talked about and treated by students and staff at our university. There was no group on campus that people expected to do less when it came to service and missions work. Yet this was the group that most immediately accepted me and my family at Cornerstone University; the men's soccer coach became one of my best friends and the players were often my lunch table companions.

In the middle of my first school year I had a chance to help lead a trip to the Dominican Republic for some guys on the Cornerstone men's soccer team. One of our student captains, Dave DeBoer, helped us connect with a community in great need on this beautiful island. As we walked through the stream of raw sewage children daily crossed on their way to school, the compassionate and courageous Spirit of God stirred in many hearts, including mine in a fresh way. We helped to move a family from a home with falling tin walls and a leaky roof to a new home that another family from Michigan had funded and built. Their large, extended family chose to put all their Christmas resources toward the building of this new home for a family in the Los Alcarrizos community. I ended up taking the men's basketball team to the same community right after school got out as we began to build a long-term relationship with this community in the Dominican Republic where God was at work doing remarkable things.

As I started my second school year at Cornerstone University, I found myself again stirred and surprised at who God chooses to use to speak on behalf of the vulnerable in our world today. This questionable bunch of college soccer players who got to know the poor on a week-long missions project on a Caribbean island decided to host an event called "Night of Nets" where they invited students and others to come watch our men's and women's soccer teams play the game that is loved all over the world. Each spectator who came was invited to pay a six-dollar admission fee that would purchase an insecticide-treated bed net for a family in sub-Saharan Africa trying to avoid the bite of a mosquito that could threaten the future of the people in their family every night. We had our largest crowd of the season by far. A gang of athletes previously deemed most likely to not care about the needs of others raised the resources in another partnership with World Vision to distribute over one thousand bed nets to families who prayed for someone to help them obtain something that would potentially save their lives.

The basketball team that wowed some Dominican fans with their three-point shooting decided to host a night called "Hoops for H2O." For this event they partnered with their hated cross-town rival to raise the funds needed to build a clean water well through a partnership with Living Water International for a school community in Kenya serving a large number of children orphaned by the HIV/ AIDS virus. Many of the students involved in our ACT:S group were rather surprised to see athletes leading the way in this response, but I knew God wasn't the least bit shocked to see some unlikely characters stepping out and caring about those He knew and loved so deeply. I've seen it happen time and time again, no matter where I go.

My prayer has been and continues to be that the words you have read will move you to ask what you can do and must do in response to the story shared in this book. I want you to know that the goal isn't to raise hundreds of thousands of dollars or travel multiple times to Africa because it has been done in another place by a group of students. Over the last three years following the period of my direct involvement with an African community I've figured out a few things that are the real takeaways from the Zambia Project:

> Responding to the needs and building relationships with the poor and the oppressed is everyone's business and you don't need the "best of the best" when it comes to students to help facilitate a meaningful response.

The size of the project does not matter. The reality of some kind of actual response stirs something deep in the heart of both the giver and receiver whether it's a new hospital or a lone goat.

There are opportunities to become involved based on one's specific interests and passions. Our global community and your local neighborhood are filled with creative and compassionate people who have set up places for you and those in your world to become involved with an issue that will grab your attention and investment.

Getting to know personally people from other cultures in their own communities and local contexts is transformational for one's faith and vision of life. A cross-cultural trip experience is the lighter fluid that often ignites a raging fire to advocate for peoples and places outside your normal life.

The time is right now to respond as many of the needs in our world demand decisive and immediate action. I believe God is waiting, the church is waiting, people in need are waiting, students are waiting, and your own soul is waiting for you to care about things that move the heart of God and the hands of Jesus in the Scriptures.

For a list of resources and ideas on how to get involved, along with some specific organizations to partner with, check out the list in the Recommended Resources or visit the book's website at www.zambiaprojectbook.com

This coming summer I am headed back to Zambia with some of these student athletes from the Cornerstone University community for a first trip to Africa from my new home in Grand Rapids. Simply put, I just can't stay away. Not because the community needs me to help them or guide them in their decisions and future direction. And not just because I want to see the new buildings and structures that I know will help transform lives for generations to come.

I can't stay away because of the moment I will experience as we drive down a rough and dusty dirt path to my little village that I call a second home. It is the moment when a mother weeps when handed the mesh net that will save her child's life. It is the moment when I am all at once overwhelmed with grief, with joy, with compassion, with deep concern, and with hope. It is the moment when I am perhaps most fully alive as I experience the vast breadth of human emotions in my heart and mind.

And it is a moment when I believe once again deep in my soul that this generation must and can and will change the paradigm and change the world's reality in the name of the One who has indeed made all things broken become whole, made all things that have grown old suddenly become new, and made all things reflect the nature and glory that only He can ultimately display to a people and a world looking to see it in the midst of their lives.

May God give us the courage to both join and release a Kingdom team of Jesus followers that does indeed turn the world and millions of lives upside down.

CHIP

RECOMMENDED RESOURCES

BOOKS

Batstone, David. *Not for Sale: The Return of the Global Slave Trade—and How We Can Fight It*. New York: HarperSanFrancisco, 2007.

Bono. *On the Move*. Nashville: Thomas Nelson, 2006.

Cantelon, James. *When God Stood Up: A Christian Response to AIDS in Africa*. Mississauga, Canada: Wiley Publishers, 2007.

Corbett, Steve, and Brian Fikkert, *When Helping Hurts: How to Alleviate Poverty without Hurting the Poor...and Yourself*. Chicago: Moody Publishers, 2009.

Greer, Peter, and Phil Smith. *The Poor Will Be Glad: Joining the Revolution to Lift the World Out of Poverty*. Grand Rapids, MI: Zondervan, 2009.

Haugen, Gary. *Good News about Injustice: A Witness of Courage in a Hurting World*. Downers Grove, IL: InterVarsity Press, 1999.

Lee, Jena and Jeremy Cowart. *Hope in the Dark*. Relevant Books, 2006.

Livermore, David. *What Can I Do?: Making a Global Difference Right Where You Are*. Grand Rapids, MI: Zondervan, 2011.

Myers, Bryant. *Walking with the Poor: Principles and Practices of Transformational Development*. Maryknoll, NY: Orbis Books, 2011.

Nolen, Stephanie. *28: Stories of AIDS in Africa*. New York: Walker & Company, 2007.

Phillips, Todd. *Get Uncomfortable: Serve the Poor. Stop Injustice. Change the World...In Jesus' Name*. Nashville: LifeWay Press, 2007.

Sachs, Jeffrey. *The End of Poverty: Economic Possibilities for Our Time*. New York: Penguin Press, 2005.

Sider, Ronald. *Rich Christians in an Age of Hunger*. Nashville: Thomas Nelson, 2005.

Stearns, Richard. *The Hole in Our Gospel*. Nashville: Thomas Nelson, 2009.

Todd, Dr. Scott. *Fast Living: How the Church Will End Extreme Poverty.* Colorado Springs: Compassion International, 2011.

Van Schooneveld, Amber. *Hope Lives: A Journey of Restoration.* Loveland, CO: Group Publishing, 2008.

Warren, Kay. *Dangerous Surrender: What Happens When You Say Yes to God.* Grand Rapids, MI: Zondervan, 2007.

Yamamori, Tetsunao, David Dageforde, and Tina Bruner, eds. *The Hope Factor: Engaging the Church in the HIV/AIDS Crisis.* Waynesboro, GA: Authentic Media, 2003.

Yankoski, Mike, and Danae Yankoski. *Zealous Love: A Practical Guide to Social Justice.* Grand Rapids, MI: Zondervan, 2009.

Yunus, Muhammad. *Banker to the Poor: Micro-Lending and the Battle Against World Poverty.* New York: PublicAffairs, 2003.

Zydek, Heather, ed. *The Revolution: A Field Manual for Changing Your World.* Relevant Books, 2006.

WEBSITES

The Bill and Melinda Gates Foundation
www.gatesfoundation.org

The Global Fund
www.theglobalfund.org

Global Issues
www.globalissues.org

Hunger and World Poverty
www.poverty.com

International Justice Mission
www.ijm.org

Kaiser Global Health
www.globalhealth.kff.org

Live 58
www.live58.org

Micah Challenge
www.micahchallenge.org

The ONE Campaign
www.one.org

The President's Emergency Plan for AIDS Relief
www.avert.org/pepfar.htm

(RED)
www.joinred.com

Tearfund
www.tearfund.org

UNAIDS
www.unaids.org

The World Bank
www.worldbank.org

World Vision
www.worldvision.org

World Vision ACT:S
www.worldvisionacts.org

DOCUMENTARIES/FILMS

58: The Film, Prospect Arts, 2011, http://live58.org/thefilm/

A Closer Walk, Worldwide Documentaries, 2003, http://www.acloserwalk.org/

Call and Response, Fair Trade Pictures, 2008.

Dear Francis, Chronicle Project, 2005, http://www.chronicleproject.org/
    dearfrancis/film.html
Invisible Children, Invisible Children, Inc., 2005, http://www.invisiblechildren.
    com/home.php

Living with Slim and *Kids Living with Slim*, Sam Kauffmann Films, 2004, 2011, http://www.samkauffmann.com/films/slim/

Miss HIV, Ethnographic Media, 2007, http://www.misshiv.com/

The Age of AIDS, PBS Frontline, 2006, http://www.pbs.org/wgbh/pages/frontline/aids/

When the Night Comes, Bobby Bailey, 2010.

Yesterday, HBO Films, 2004, http://www.hbo.com/films/yesterday/

ORGANIZATIONS TO PARTNER WITH

Bright Hope International
www.brighthope.org
Local Church Based Holistic Ministry Partnerships

Compassion International
www.compassion.com
Child Sponsorship Programs, AIDS/Malaria Response Initiatives

International Justice Mission
www.ijm.org
Human Rights and Justice Work in Global Contexts

Living Water International
www.water.cc
Clean Water Wells and Projects in Global Contexts

Opportunity International
www.opportunity.org
Microfinance Loans

World Bicycle Relief
worldbicyclerelief.org
Empowering Global Development through the Power of Bicycle

World Vision
www.worldvision.org
Caregiver Kits, Child Sponsorship, Community Partnerships,
Christmas Catalog Items

NOTES

[1] Ephesians 3:20, NIV.

[2] Psalm 140:12, NIV.

[3] Proverbs 28:27, NLT.

[4] James 2:5, NLT.

[5] Proverbs 22:2, NLT.

[6] Robert Coleman, *The Master Plan of Evangelism* (Grand Rapids, MI: Baker Books, 1998), 29–31, 35–36, 38–39.

[7] Ephesians 3:16, 20, NIV.

[8] Jeremy Taylor, *The Rule and Exercises of Holy Living* (London: R. Royston, 1650).

[9] Andy Stanley, *Visioneering* (Sisters, OR: Multnomah Publishers, 1999), 17, 19, 25, 26, 55, 56, 57.

[10] William Blake, *Auguries of Innocence* (1806).

[11] Acts 2:43, 4:33, NIV.

[12] *Field of Dreams*, directed by Phil Alden Robinson (Universal City, CA: Universal Studios, 1989).

[13] Bryant Myers, *Walking with the Poor* (Maryknoll, NY: Orbis Books, 2011).

[14] Luke 5:8, NIV.

[15] Matthew 22:37-39, NLT.

[16] John 13:35, ESV.

[17] Joshua 24:15, ESV.

[18] Dallas Willard, *The Divine Conspiracy: Rediscovering our Hidden Life in God*, (San Francisco, CA: HarperSanFrancisco, 1998).

[19] Robert Fulghum, *All I Really Need to Know I Learned in Kindergarten* (New York: Villard Books, 1990), 6–7.

[20] James 1:27, NIV.

[21] Matthew 14:14, NIV.

[22] Bono, 54th National Prayer Breakfast Address, Hilton Washington Hotel, Feb 2, 2006.

[23] 1 John 3:17, THE MESSAGE.

[24] Micah 6·8, NIV.

[25] Proverbs 3:27, NLT.

[26] Genesis 1:27, 28, 31, NIV.

[27]Njongonkulu Ndungane, *A World with a Human Face: A Voice from Africa* (Cape Town, South Africa: David Philip Publishers, 2003).

[28]Matthew 6:10, NIV.

[29]Colossians 1:19-20, NIV.

[30]N. T. Wright, *Colossians and Philemon* (Downers Grove, IL: InterVarsity Press, 1986), 79–80.

[31]Rob Bell, quoted in *The Poverty and Justice Bible* (New York: American Bible Society, 2009).

[32]My goal in this chapter hasn't been to provide a complete and systematic theological analysis of these themes in Scripture. There are several other books and authors who have tackled this topic with great skill and biblical clarity that have been incredible resources for me in my own journey toward understanding how the call to biblically engage with God's heart for justice and compassion inspires me to action and response to the needs I know about and discover in our world today. Books like *Rich Christians in an Age of Hunger* by Ronald Sider, *Christianity and the Social Crisis* by Walter Rauschenbusch, *Walking with the Poor: Principles and Practices of Transformational Development* by Bryant L. Myers, *Good News about Injustice* by Gary Haugen, and *Generous Justice* by Timothy Keller are just some of the fantastic resources available for you to more deeply examine, question, and consider the biblical truths present in Scripture concerning the issues of poverty and justice.

[33]John 9:1-3, 6-7, NIV.

[34]Matthew 25:34-40, NLT.

[35]Philippians 4:19, NIV.

[36]Matthew 6:21, NIV.

[37]John Stott, *The Cross of Christ* (Downers Grove, IL: InterVarsity Press, 2006), 335–36.

[38]Matthew 5:3-10, NIV.

[39]Isaiah 58:6-7, 10, NLT.

ABOUT THE AUTHOR

Chip Huber serves as the Dean of Student Engagement at Cornerstone University in Grand Rapids, MI. You can read more of his thoughts at **chiphuber.blogspot.com** or follow him on Twitter **@chiphuber.**

For more information about this book please visit the book's website at: **zambiaprojectbook.com.**